Everybody Ought to Know
Today's Current Events Foretold Thousands of Years Ago

Everybody Ought to Know

Everybody Ought to Know
Today's Current Events Foretold Thousands of Years Ago

Dan Gamwell

Everybody Ought to Know

Everybody Ought to Know
Today's Current Events Foretold Thousands of Years Ago
Copyright © 2020 by Dan Gamwell – Revision 07052025

All rights reserved. No part of this book may be reproduced, stored in a retrieval system, or transmitted in any form or by any means electronic or mechanical without written permission from the author.

978-1-7347200-5-1

Dedication

This book is dedicated to you for your sense of and interest in the consequential.

Everybody Ought to Know

Table of Contents

-Prologue-

Dedication v
Foreword.. 1
Introduction.. 3
Let's Set the Stage.. 7
Some Context.. 9
Bible Prophecy vs Prognostication........................ 11
What If God Accurately Predicted the Future?..... 23
By The Way... 27

-Prophecies-

The Jews a Blessing to the World 29
Jews Dispersed Worldwide....................................... 33
Israel Reborn... 37
Return to Never Leave Again................................... 45
Two Nations to Become One 47
Israel to be Formed in One Day.............................. 49
Israel Would Include Jerusalem 51
Jerusalem: A Political Problem................................ 57
Israel Renowned For Its Agriculture 59
Israel to be Militarily Formidable........................... 65
Curse on Chorazin, Bethsaida and Capernaum... 69
What's the Big Deal with the Jews?........................ 71
Prophecy Revealed in End Times 83
Many Will Rush Here and There 87
Knowledge Will Increase 89
Wars, Famines & Earthquakes................................. 91
Gospel Preached Worldwide 101
Russia in the Middle East.. 107
Worldwide Simultaneous Observation 113
Commerce Controlled Centrally........................... 115

Mount of Olives to Split in Half 119
Increase in Sin, Immorality and Violence 121
Increase in Materialism 131
Increase in Christian Martyrdom 137
Population Explosion 141

-Epilogue-

So What? 143
Think About This 151
Final Thoughts 175
Closing Notes 203
Acknowledgments 205

Foreword

Dan Gamwell has written an outstanding book about Bible prophecy that is well worth reading. He writes with a breezy, enthusiastic style that makes what he has to say exciting to read.

The author points to currently fulfilling prophecy as absolute evidence of the integrity of God's Word and God's sovereignty in history. He then provides a sweeping overview of the signs of the times that point to the Lord's imminent return.

He concludes with a passionate plea for unbelievers to take seriously the evidence of fulfilled prophecy as proof of Jesus' claim to be the only way to God. Overall, the book is a spiritual feast.

-Dr. David R. Reagan

> Dr. Reagan is the author of many books in addition to innumerable magazine articles. He is also the founder of Lamb & Lion Ministries.

Everybody Ought to Know

Introduction

It is one thing to be aware of the historic details of ancient prophecies that are currently taking place as predicted. It is another thing, though, to understand their implication and significance to the course of human existence. Certainly, we want to know the *what* of these ancient prophecies, but more important still would be the *why*. To that end we will need to spend several short chapters to develop the context for what we are about to see.

Imagine you were God and wanted to communicate your heart, your ways, your plans, and your expectations to human beings whom you had created out of love for the express purpose of sharing an intimacy with them. Suppose you knew that some of them didn't even believe that you existed while others had biased and distorted ideas about you that were based on opinion, conjecture, and ever-changing social conventions. Yet still, because of your sincere love for them, you felt compelled to seek them out for a personal relationship. How would you do that?

Well, if you were as smart as God, you would do several things. You would send many people to tell them, and you would establish the credibility of those messengers with miracles. This God did with all the prophets and spiritual leaders that we read about throughout Scripture.

You would also explicitly communicate all your counsel, concern, and grand plans for them in a book like the Bible.

You would do more than that, though. You would go and tell them yourself. That is exactly what God the Son, Jesus, did when He was born of a virgin and lived and taught here on Earth.

Now, imagine for a second that you were the devil and wanted to thwart everything God was trying to do with these people. How would you do that? Well, if you were as treacherous and devious as the devil, besides doing everything you could do to appeal to their depraved nature, (which resulted from man's choice to reject God and which then brought sin and its consequences into the world) you would inspire a flood of distracting messages to confuse the people. That is exactly what the devil has done with the cacophony of chaotic religious ideas out there.

If you were God, however, you would have a distinct advantage in this war of messages, because you would know the future. So, your ace in this battle would be the ability to tell the future in order to distinguish your message from all the counterfeits. Enter—currently fulfilling Bible prophecy.

What is currently fulfilling Bible prophecy? It is recent and current world events that were prophesied two thousand years ago, or more, to occur at this time in history. By *this time in history* I mean our current era. Basically, the time starting from May 14th, 1948. (We will discuss why that date a little later.)

There is past fulfilled prophecy whose realization we can read about in Scripture. There is also future, still unfulfilled, prophecy. But currently fulfilling Bible prophecies are events in modern history that you are aware of without maybe realizing that they were prophesied in the Bible to happen at this particular time in history. Many of these prophetic events you are reading about in news headlines every day.

Currently fulfilling Bible prophecy is prophecy that you cannot deny as you watch the fulfillment before your very eyes. Currently fulfilling Bible prophecy leaves little room to dispute the genuineness of the Bible.

We live in a time when more prophecies are being fulfilled than perhaps at any other time in history, with the exception of the time of Christ. Currently fulfilling Bible prophecy is proof positive of the accuracy and miraculous nature of the Bible. It is irrefutable evidence that cannot be ignored by an honest person. It endorses the message of the Bible, which offers hope to the world.

Currently fulfilling Bible prophecy is possibly the strongest corroboration of the Bible that exists today. It offers confirmation and secure sanctuary to the believer and compelling testimony to the unbeliever.

Everybody Ought to Know

Let's Set the Stage

A word concerning predictions about "the end of the world."

A handful of people have made irresponsible predictions over the last several hundred years. Well-intentioned or not, it is hard to imagine such foolishness in light of the fact that the Bible clearly states in Matthew 24:36, "*However,* **no one knows the day or hour** *when these things will happen, not even the angels in heaven or the Son himself. Only the Father knows."*

Such proclamations have served the devil's ends very well as they created confusion, not to mention scorn for the Bible-believing community as these dates came and went without the predicted Rapture or "end of the world".

Don't fall for the devil's deception

The devil is so clever. He throws voices out there crying "wolf", or "Jesus is coming at such and such a time" in this case. When the prediction fails, people become skeptical and lose confidence in the message of the Bible. That's what the devil wants. For want of discernment or for lack of knowledge, many people don't know what to believe and so ignore the subject altogether.

Just as in the well-known Aesop fable, people become desensitized to the message because of those who venture beyond what the Bible says and preach conjecture as Biblical truth. Don't forfeit the advantage of knowing prophecy because of the mismanagement of the subject by some.

It's not complicated

Nearly one third of the Bible is prophecy. The fulfillment of many of the prophecies have already occurred. Many prophecies, however, are being fulfilled in our generation. And, of course, there are others that have yet to be fulfilled, although that number is continually shrinking as prophecies move to the "completed" column.

Our focus in this book is only on prophecy that is currently being fulfilled in our day as opposed to future, still unfulfilled prophecy. There is no room for dispute, here, because we are not attempting to prognosticate the future, but rather to only speak of what already is. And so, there is no reason to fear the subject, either, because again, we are not attempting to divine the future, but rather to only speak of what already is.

In 1933 the movie "Duck Soup" was released. There is a well-known line from it where Chico Marx, dressed as Groucho Marx, says, "Who you gonna believe? Me or your lying eyes?" Of course, your eyes don't lie. You can believe your eyes as we go through the Bible prophecies being fulfilled today, and you can see them for yourself.

Some Context

There was a time, before May 14th, 1948, when most of the end time prophecies seemed too inconceivable for many people to believe. That date, which we will soon discuss, began a new era of fulfilled Bible prophecy. But before that...

Two hundred years ago, what did people think of a prophecy that spoke of the entire world being able to simultaneously watch the same event? To unbelievers, it was a preposterous thought that could only be accepted by religious fanatics with no sense of reality. But that was then, and this is now.

Two hundred years ago, what did people think of a prophecy that said that the Jews would all return to Israel when there was no country for them to return to at the time? The place where Israel had existed thousands of years earlier was by then just a dusty corner of the vast Ottoman Empire. There was no way the Muslims were going to concede anything to the Jews. Besides, the Jews were spread all over the world with many different languages and cultures. But that was then, and this is now.

> *The place Israel had existed thousands of years earlier was by then just a dusty corner of the vast Ottoman Empire.*

Hats off to these folks

Let me take a moment to pay tribute to those faithful and humble Christians of yester-year. They read these prophecies that sounded like science fiction, yet they still stood courageously by the Bible, enduring the scoffing and insults from those who thought them laughable, even contemptible.

I am reminded of Thomas, the disciple. When he was told that Jesus had risen from the dead, he said that he would not believe until he saw Jesus for himself. A week later Jesus presented himself to Thomas and said these words that you can read in John 20:29, *"Because you have seen me, you have believed; blessed are those who have not seen and yet have believed."* Currently fulfilling Bible prophecy makes believing easy today.

For the last 2,000 years it took real faith to believe. Today however, not so much. Currently fulfilling Bible prophecy removes any doubt that the message is true. But will people be **honest** enough to admit what their eyes see as they watch the fulfillment of these ancient prophecies unfold before them? Will they be **humble** enough to accept the message of the book that tells the future, which calls for submission to a loving God that wants only the very best for them?

Bible Prophecy vs Prognostication

No one should ever confuse Biblical prophecy with what I call *Nostradamus-speak*. *Nostradamus-speak* is cryptic, unintelligible writings that can only be associated with events in hindsight after incidents have already occurred. Only after events have occurred can any attempt be made to make a connection. For example, here is a Nostradamus quatrain.

Century 1 Quatrain 81

Nine will be set apart from the human flock
Separated from judgement and counsel:
Their fate to be determined on departure
Great blame, to the other great praise.

That, my friend, was supposed to be a prediction of the Challenger disaster when seven astronauts perished. Oh, it wasn't obvious to you either? By the way, the Challenger carried only seven astronauts, not nine.

Why didn't someone warn NASA beforehand of the danger if this is so obvious? As you can see, it is only after an event that an attempt could ever be made to make some connection. Even so, it seems a ridiculous stretch.

For fun, let's look at one more.

Century 6 Quatrain 97

At forty-five degrees the sky will burn,
Fire to approach the great new city:
In an instant a great scattered flame will leap up,
When one will want to demand proof of the Normans.

So, you didn't realize that was a description of the 9/11 destruction of the Twin Towers in New York City? Neither did I. In fact, neither did they, until after the fact. And why is this not a description of the great Chicago fire of 1871 or any of the cities firebombed during World War II? You see, it can be anything you want it to be.

Stubbornness in the face of truth

After sharing currently fulfilling Bible prophecy with a young man whose mom had warned me was an avowed hater of anything godly, he said he was unimpressed because Nostradamus could also tell the future. After a few questions it was obvious to both of us that he knew nothing of Nostradamus or his nonsensical writings. He was just looking for an excuse not to believe.

When people don't want to believe, they can use anything as an excuse. For example, one might say that though Hitler was responsible for more than 50 million deaths, "He couldn't have been that bad because I saw him kiss a baby."

When a person is prejudicially selective of the facts that they are willing to consider, they can miss the truth by a wide margin and convince themselves of anything they want to believe. However, currently fulfilling Bible prophecy makes it harder to do so. Still, though, the person determined to believe only what they want to believe, always will anyway.

Such people remind me of a patient in psychiatric care who was convinced that he was dead. The psychiatrist, while trying to convince him that he was alive, asked him if dead people bleed. The patient answered, "Of course they don't." The psychiatrist reaffirmed his answer. Then he pricked the patient's finger. When, indeed, he bled, the patient exclaimed, "Why dead people *do* bleed."

While some people cannot be reasoned with, currently fulfilling Bible prophecy serves to make their stubbornness and rejection of God obvious. Their derision for God is exposed by their irrational disinterest in Biblical prophetic facts. They can't explain how a book can so accurately predict the future, but they don't want to think about it, either. Their closemindedness towards spiritual things becomes glaringly conspicuous in the bright light of currently fulfilling Bible prophecy. Their intolerance for God is laid bare.

> *A person determined to believe only what they want to believe, always will. They don't know the truth, but they don't care.*

I also bring up Nostradamus to draw attention to the contrasting clarity and detail of the Biblical prophecies we will be looking at, compared to the indecipherable and meaningless incoherence of Nostradamus and other similarly confusing prognostications that can be interpreted to mean anything you want.

Who else can tell the future besides God?

The devil can occasionally tell the future just like you and I can occasionally tell the future. He just can't be 100% accurate, just like you and I can't be, either. Let me explain.

I can tell you that tomorrow a handsome and charming guy will mow my front yard. How do I know that? I know that because I plan to mow my lawn tomorrow. I make plans all the time, and sometimes they actually pan out. But often they don't.

My plans can get preempted by all kinds of circumstances from weather to health to priority changes to Pam, my wife.

You see? What is to stop the devil from predicting something that he plans to do? Like with you and me, he hasn't the power to always do what he wants to do. But he can be right sometimes, when God doesn't trump his plans. The Bible tells us that God has, for a limited period, conceded limited authority to the devil. I John 5:19 says, *"...the world around us is under the control of the evil one."* And 2 Corinthians 4:4 says, *"The god of this world* (the devil) *has blinded the minds of the unbelievers."*

Magic shows are fun. The magician's tricks appear to be supernatural. In every way they seem impossible to us. But the truth is, we know that they all have a simple explanation. We just don't know what that explanation is, because we can't see what goes on behind the curtain.

A person goes to a fortune teller and is amazed when they hear things about their past that the medium could not have possibly known. The foolish gull puts their money and their trust where they never should. They don't see the unromantic truth behind the curtain. If they could, they would find it unnerving and chilling. You see, a person's past is no mystery to the devil. The devil can share that information with his agents. A person without a deep personal relationship with the Lord is easily seduced by such simple trickery. The devil knows the past. He can only guess at the future, just like we all can.

God knows this and gives us severe warnings about consulting the devil's "prophets". He warns against it from one end of the Bible to the other. He warns us because He loves us, and He knows there are ugly consequences for those that consult the devil's team. Here is one such warning in the 5th book of the Bible: Deuteronomy 18:10-12 says, *"Do not let your people practice fortune-telling, or use sorcery, or interpret omens, or engage in witchcraft, or cast spells, or function as mediums or psychics, or call forth the spirits of the dead.* **Anyone who does these things is detestable to the LORD."**

Many other verses communicate the same sentiment. Consider Leviticus 20:6 that says, *"If any of you go for advice to people who consult the spirits of the dead, I will turn against you..."*

A person who consults these mediums is flirting with the enemy. Being unaware about these things can put a person in an awfully bad place. It can put them outside of God's protection, and it can make them dangerously vulnerable to the demonic without even knowing it until the consequences are felt. God wants to save us from those consequences. The book that tells the future predicts a sad ending for those who ignore His warning.

How are you supposed to know the difference?

A person who has a genuine relationship with Jesus will be able to tell the difference between emissaries of God and emissaries of the devil. Someone without a genuine relationship with Jesus may not find it so easy to tell the difference.

In 2 Corinthians 11:13-14 we read this, *"These people are false representatives for God. They are **deceitful workers who disguise themselves as representatives of Christ**. ...**Even Satan disguises himself as an angel of light**."* It is not enough that a medium speak of God or present themself as very spiritual, because the evil one is adept at that con. Just below I'll describe how to easily spot these imposters.

God repeatedly and emphatically warns against association with fortune-tellers, mediums, psychics, and the like. Here is an admonition from I John 4:1-3 that reads, *"Beloved, do not believe every spirit, but test the spirits to see whether they are from God, for many false prophets have gone out into the world. By this you know the Spirit of God: every spirit that confesses that Jesus Christ has come in the flesh is from God, and every spirit that does not confess Jesus is not from God."*

> *2 Corinthians 11:13*
> *"These people are false representative for God. They are deceitful workers who disguise themselves as representatives of Christ."*

There are some "tells" for discerning the truth. The previous verse explains that the emissaries of Satan, though they appear to be angels of light, cannot bring themselves to say that the Jesus of the Bible is God in the flesh and that salvation is only through Him. You will also find that they do not promote holy living according to God's standards as described in the Bible. You won't find them hanging out with other people that love Jesus, either. Nor do they promote serious Bible study. Most importantly, they don't urge one to have a personal relationship with Jesus Christ. And finally, their activities are almost always related to personal gain. In other words, be sure to bring your money.

In Jesus' description in Matthew 24 of what to expect just prior to His return, consider this warning in verse 24, *"For false messiahs and **false prophets will appear and perform great signs and wonders** to deceive, if it were possible, even believers."*

This is no time to be unaware of the spiritual battles that we may unknowingly be involved in, as Ephesians 6:12 tells us, *"For our struggle is not against flesh and blood, but against the rulers, against the authorities, **against the powers of this dark world and against the spiritual forces of evil** in the spirit realm."*

How recklessly naive it is to not realize that the difficult circumstances we wrestle with every day have very real spiritual implications. It should be no wonder then, that so many people seem to be "yanked every

> *How recklessly naive it is to not realize that the difficult circumstances we wrestle with every day, have very real spiritual implications.*

which way but loose" by their circumstances for lack of Bible based spiritual awareness.

Unfortunately, they are clueless about the warning of the previous verse. They are unaware that evil in the spiritual realm can reach out and touch them in ways that won't be at all obvious to them. And it is even more likely to happen when they make themselves vulnerable by engaging the dark side.

Deception in different forms.

Forgive me for diverting a bit from the topic of this chapter, but since we are talking about deception, there is one other naivety I should mention. Many people foolishly lump all churches into the same basket, thinking they are all the same. They are the same like a cobra and a garter snake are the same. If you don't know your snakes, then let me say that all churches are the same like *up* and *down* are the same.

I remember, once, while eating some pistachios I came across a most bitter one. I thought to myself that if that had been the first I ever tasted, I'd probably not eat another all my life. I fear some people have had that experience with church, and now they have no interest at all.

Attending church can be a little like taking medicine for many people; some churches are just about as fun too. But when taking medicine, not just any medicine will do. The wrong medicine can kill you.

One of my first jobs was working in a hospital pharmacy nearly 50 years ago. I once dispensed the wrong drug that had a very similar name to the correct one. Fortunately, the nurse caught the mistake and saved the patient's life. (Mine, too!)

You need to know what you're doing when handling medicines because of the negative consequences of making a mistake. Much more important are the negative eternal consequences of a mistake in church selection. To think they are all the same is as callow as thinking all drugs are the same.

There exists the absurd notion that any faith is a good faith. Wouldn't an honest person have to admit that truth matters? You can't just believe whatever you like and expect good results.

Consider this silly declaration based on wrong thinking: on January 21st, 1933, Syria's Prime Minister, Haqqi al Azm, banned the yo-yo because it was thought to be responsible for the severe cold and disastrous drought that was affecting their cattle. This Syrian Prime Minister truly believed that yo-yos affected the climate. His "truly believing" did not make it so, however.

Truth matters. Do you think that a man who self-identifies as a woman can avoid the danger of prostate cancer when he is older? Of course not! Things are what they are, not what you choose to call them.

Ronald Reagan once asked, "If you count a dog's tail as a leg, how many legs does it have." When the answer came back as, "Five," he said, "No, only four. You can call a tail a leg but it is still a tail." This seems fundamental, yet many people think that whatever they believe about God and the hereafter will come true for them. Will death not bring a rude awakening to such folks?

Protect yourself from deception.

Let me tell you the most elementary way to know the difference between a church that will do you harm and one that will do you good. Avoid any church that promotes itself as being the exclusive way to heaven, instead of promoting Jesus as the exclusive way to heaven. In the only book that tells the future, Jesus said that He is *"the way, the truth and the life"* and that no one will get into heaven except through Him. He never mentioned a particular church.

> *Avoid any church that promotes itself as being the exclusive way to heaven, instead of promoting Jesus as the exclusive way.*

Another very basic warning would be to avoid any church that fails to encourage and equip you to study the Bible so that you can discover its truths for yourself.

Need I even mention how foolish it is to think that all religions lead one to the same god? Discover how each religion's god is described and you will immediately expose irreconcilable differences with what the Bible says about God.

> *Jesus said that He is "the way, the truth and the life." He never mentioned a particular church.*

Man without God.

The world seems on the verge of a melt-down as the problems of politics, health, and economy merge into an unmanageable mess. People, societies, and governments are becoming more and more overwhelmed with insurmountable problems. As they look for solutions in political parties, science, education, and regulations, they willingly spend trillions in their search. They are desperately prepared to try anything—but God.

Look around you. Tell me if "man without God" is doing a good job. Tell me if "man without God" is handling government responsibilities well. Tell me if "man without God" is handling race relations well. Tell me if "man without God" is doing a good job of raising the next generation. Tell me if "man without God" is managing world affairs well.

But you say, "Yeah, but 'man **with** God' has done some bad things, too. Like the Crusades, and slavery, and religious intolerance." But you would be wrong, because those things and many other bad things like them were all done by "man with religion." That's a very different and dangerous thing. I cannot advocate religion. I can, however, advocate a relationship between you and your creator—God.

When you see the miracles of currently fulfilled Bible prophecy in upcoming chapters, I hope you are convinced to pursue that relationship.

Everybody Ought to Know

What If God Accurately Predicted the Future?

Despite severe opposition, Michael Burry, a hedge fund manager, accurately predicted the 2008 financial crisis precipitated by a collapsing housing market which he wisely anticipated. Needless to say, though previously criticized, he came to be respected and sought after.

Throughout the Bible God attempted to persuade mankind to trust Him by using prophecy that was being fulfilled to show how to know what was true and what wasn't. After all, only God knows the future.

God tells us the future so we will know it too, and who to trust. Jesus told His disciples about Judas' betrayal before it happened in order to further convince them that He was, indeed, the Messiah. John 13:19 says, "*I tell you this **beforehand**, so that when it happens you will believe that I Am the Messiah.*"

Again, Jesus told the disciples of His impending ascension to heaven, before it occurred, to offer even more evidence that He spoke the truth. John 14:29 says this, "*I have told you these things **before they happen** so that when they do happen, you will believe.*"

How about the prophecy in the second chapter of John that persuaded the disciples to trust Jesus when it was fulfilled in their day? John 2:19-22 says, *"Jesus answered them, 'Destroy this temple, and I will raise it again in three days.' The Jews replied, 'It has taken forty-six years to build this temple, and you are going to raise it in three days?' But the temple He had spoken of was his body. After He was raised from the dead, His disciples recalled what he had said.* **Then they believed the Scripture and the words that Jesus had spoken.***"*

> *John 14:29*
> *"I have told you these things before they happen so that when they do happen, you will believe."*

Then again, in Matthew 24, Jesus described many things that would happen towards the end of this age, preceding His return. In verse 25 He says, *"Please notice that I am telling you these things* **before they happen**.*"* He conspicuously asks us all to notice that He spoke these things prophetically.

We see the same thing in the Old Testament as well. In foretelling the ultimate deliverance of Israel from its oppressors, God pointed out that when it finally came to pass, they would have to believe Him because He had foretold it. Isaiah 52:6 says, *"Therefore my people will know my name; therefore, in that day they will know that* **it is I who foretold it**. *Yes, it is I."*

Today we see that the final deliverance of Israel has already begun with the Jews returning to Israel, just as the prophecies foretold.

In Isaiah 41 and 42, God was trying to persuade the Jews to desert their idols and return to Him. Isaiah 41:21 says, *"Go ahead, make a case for your idols..."* In verse 23, God speaks to those idols, with tongue in cheek, *"Yes, tell us what will occur in the days ahead. Then we will know you are gods. In fact, just do something—good or bad! Do anything that might amaze or frighten us."* Then He contrasts Himself with those lifeless idols in Isaiah 42:9 when He says, *"Everything I prophesied has come true, and now I will prophecy again.* **I will tell you the future before it happens."**

Again, in Isaiah 43, God tells the Jews exactly what to expect in the future. In verse 9 He challenges the false gods of that time by saying, *"Which of their gods foretold this and the other things occurring right now? Let them bring in their witnesses to prove they were right."*

Then, in verse 12, He drives the point home by saying, "**I have revealed** *and saved and proclaimed—I, and not some foreign god among you."*

Of course, there are many other such references where God tried to get people to pay attention by showing them miracles. Not to belabor the point, let me share just one more. In Deuteronomy 4:35 Moses was referring to miracles that God had done when he said, *"You were shown these things so that you might know that the LORD is God; besides Him there is no other."*

Today, God is doing the same with currently fulfilling Bible prophecy. After all, how else could you hope to find the truth among so many religious messages in a world with so many theological ideas?

In the following chapters we will look at these ancient prophecies that are miraculously coming to pass in our day. Then we will consider their importance in several key chapters at the end of this book.

Now, fasten your seat belt!

By The Way...

Notice this casual prophecy made by Jesus in Matthew 26:6-13. *"While Jesus was in Bethany in the home of a man known as Simon the Leper, a woman came to him with an alabaster jar of very expensive perfume, which she poured on his head as he was reclining at the table. ...Jesus said to [those present]...'I tell you the truth,* **wherever this gospel is preached throughout the world, what she has done will also be told, in memory of her.'"**

Prophecy Fulfilled The words that Jesus spoke did not vaporize into the air that day. Here we are 2,000 years later and you just read those words yourself, fulfilling that prophecy for the gazillionth time.

There are many other such incidental prophecies throughout the Bible that have been and are being fulfilled just like that one. However, the prophecies, here recounted, are predominantly limited to those of major political, social, economic or military significance to the world.

The Jews a Blessing to the World

In the following chapters, one of the things we will be considering is the incredible miracle that is the existence of Israel today. That probably does not sound that incredible, though, to someone less aware of world history—particularly, the history of the Jewish nation. So, I will occasionally intertwine a brief summary of historical facts that will further accentuate these astonishing prophecies.

While many of the currently fulfilling Bible prophecies that we will consider have nothing to do with the Jews, some of them do concern the Jews and Israel. Let us start with this. Where did the Jews come from? We find the answer in Genesis 12:1-3, *"Now the Lord said to Abram, 'Go from your country and your kindred and your father's house to the land that I will show you. And I will make of you a great nation, and I will bless you and make your name great, so that you will be a blessing. I will bless those who bless you, and him who dishonors you I will curse, and **in you all the families of the earth shall be blessed.**'"* Abram was the father of the Jewish nation. (NOTE: God later changed Abram's name to Abraham.)

Abraham had only one son by his wife Sarah. His name was Isaac. God then repeated to Isaac the promise that He had made to his father, Abraham. Genesis 26:3-4 says this, *"Sojourn in this land, and I will be with you and will bless you, for to you and to your offspring I will give all these lands, and I will establish the oath that I swore to*

Abraham your father. I will multiply your offspring as the stars of heaven and will give to your offspring all these lands. And **in your offspring, all the nations of the earth shall be blessed.**"

Abraham's son, Isaac, had a son named Jacob. Underscoring the prophecy, God repeated the promise a third time to Abraham's grandson, Jacob. Genesis 28:13-14 reads, *"I am the LORD, the God of Abraham your father and the God of Isaac. The land on which you lie I will give to you and to your offspring. Your offspring shall be like the dust of the earth, and you shall spread abroad to the west and to the east and to the north and to the south, and* **in you and your offspring shall all the families of the earth be blessed.**"

I ask you, has God blessed all the families on earth through the Jews like He promised three times to Abraham, Isaac, and Jacob? Well, let's see.

Prophecy Fulfilled. First of all, let's remind ourselves that Jesus was Jewish. Next, it would be helpful to know that Hebrews 9:22 says, *"Without the shedding of blood there is no forgiveness of sins."* Only because of His birth, death, and resurrection does humanity have any hope of heaven and protection from the eternal consequences of sin. That is because Jesus, being perfect (sinless), was the ultimate sacrifice for sin which was anticipated throughout the Old Testament by example of the animal sacrifices. The opportunity for the salvation of men's souls from the eternal consequences of their sin is the

> *First of all, let's remind ourselves that Jesus was Jewish*

greatest way that God has blessed humanity through the Jewish nation.

But that is not all. Not by a long shot. The percentage of Jews who have won Nobel prizes for things that have greatly benefited mankind, is quite noteworthy. Since 1901, when the award was first established, the Jewish Virtual Library reports that approximately 193 of the 855 honorees, up to this point, have been Jewish. That means that 22% of all Nobel prizes have been awarded to a people group that represents less than 0.2% of the global population.

If the Jews had won the same percentage of Nobel prizes that their population represents, they should have won only 1.7—not 193!

It is truly, truly a remarkable currently fulfilling Bible prophecy, that 0.2% of the world's population has produced 22% of the greatest advancements, innovations, and discoveries to bless humanity in the last 120 years. This is in clear fulfillment of God's promise to bless all the nations of the world through the Jews; and is despite a worldwide prejudice against them that included the genocidal horrors of the Holocaust.

> *22% of all Nobel prizes have been awarded to Jews which represent less than 0.2% of the global population.*

Has God blessed humanity through the Jewish nation? Obviously!

Everybody Ought to Know

Jews Dispersed Worldwide

We need a little history to fully appreciate this next fulfilled prophecy. Abraham's grandson, Jacob, had 12 sons. They lived in Egypt for just over 400 years, during which time they multiplied into several million. They had lots and lots of kids. Do the math.

After many years, the Egyptians became alarmed by the number of Israelites (descendants of Jacob whose name God changed to Israel) living among them, so they enslaved them. Enter—Moses.

After quite a confrontation with Pharoah, Moses led them out of Egypt into the Promised Land—the land promised to their forefathers, Abraham, Isaac, and Jacob over 400 years earlier. Before they entered the Promised Land, which is basically Israel today, God promised to bless them like crazy if they would stay faithful to Him and not be seduced to follow the idols of the land they were about to enter.

We can read some of the promised blessing in Deuteronomy 28:1-8 which says, *"If you fully obey the LORD your God and carefully keep all his commands that I am giving you today, the LORD your God will set you high above all the nations of the world. You will experience all these blessings if you obey the LORD your God: Your towns and your fields will be blessed. Your children and your crops will be blessed. The offspring of your herds and flocks will be blessed. Your fruit baskets and breadboards will be blessed. Wherever you go and whatever you do, you will be blessed. The LORD will conquer your enemies when they attack you. They will attack you from one direction, but they will scatter from you in seven! The LORD will guarantee a blessing on everything you do and will fill your storehouses with grain. The LORD your God will bless you in the land he is giving you."*

But God warned them repeatedly that if they strayed from following Him and adopted the disgusting practices of the idol worshippers of the region, He would not only take away the blessings, but add curses instead. One of the horrific and disgusting practices of these pagans was child sacrifice by fire.

God warned them that He would take away everything He had given them, including the land itself. Deuteronomy 28:20-68 is just one place, of many, that this warning can be read. Let's read verses 63-64, *"You will be torn from the land you are about to enter and occupy.* **For the LORD will scatter you among all the nations** *from one end of the earth to the other."*

Prophecy Fulfilled. God said that He would disperse the Jews throughout the earth if they turned their back on Him. Boy, did they ever turn their back on Him and boy did God ever scatter them. God was patient with them for hundreds of years during which time He sent them many, many prophets to remind them over and over of the consequences they would have to suffer. They paid the prophets no mind as they indulged in all the evil practices of the surrounding idol worshippers. Yes, they even sacrificed their babies in fire to their idols.

God had commanded the Jews to rid the land of these people who deserved God's judgement for their abominable practices. He warned them that these idol-worshippers would one day be their downfall if they failed in this directive. Well, the Jews failed, and these pagan idol-worshippers did indeed prove to be the downfall of the entire Jewish nation. They ended up losing everything.

They failed God, and who can deny that they were dispersed throughout the earth as God promised they would be? Today there are between 14 and 23 million Jews on earth, depending how you choose to identify them. If we use the lower number, which represents full-blooded Jews, you are looking at a number that roughly equals the population of Cuba. Yet, you can find Jews here, there, and everywhere from Asia to Africa to South America, North America, and Europe. Beyond question they have been dispersed throughout the nations of the earth and have been without a country until May 14th, 1948—just after World War II.

> *He warned them that these idol-worshippers would one day be their downfall*

Of even greater significance is the fact that Jews have retained their ethnic and cultural identity even after dispersal into multiple cultures and languages the world over and without a homeland for two thousand years.

Everybody Ought to Know

Israel Reborn

I have made the comment, more than once, that many of the Bible prophecies being fulfilled today were prophesied to be fulfilled at this particular time in history. If you were wondering just how we could know that, you have a legitimate question. After all, does the Bible say that technology will increase when a certain president is in office? Or that world-wide commerce would be centrally controlled by a certain year? Of course not.

We can know that now is the time for many of these prophecies to be fulfilled because the Bible mentions them in conjunction with the fulfillment of another prophecy—the return of the Jews to Israel. Which is in turn mentioned in conjunction with Christ return to this planet. For example, in a later chapter we will specifically look at earthquakes before and after Israel became a nation. They are astounding statistics that must jolt the attention of any thoughtful person.

> *We know that now is the time for these prophecies because the Bible mentions them in conjunction with the return of the Jews to Israel.*

We have already seen the fulfillment of God's promise to disperse the Jews after they had completely immersed themselves in pagan worship and culture. But because of His promises to Abraham, Isaac, and Jacob, the forefathers of the Jews, God said that He would one day bring them back to Israel. This is a promise and prophecy repeated again and again in the Old Testament. We will look at several accounts of this prophecy.

Consider Isaiah 11:12 which says, "*He will raise a flag among the nations and* **assemble the exiles of Israel.** *He will* **gather the scattered people of Judah from the ends of the earth**." (Note: Israel and Judah both refer to the Jewish nation, since the Jews were divided into the two kingdoms of Israel and Judah during the reign of King Solomon's son, Rehoboam.)

Now, we will consider the Ezekiel 37 account of this amazing and seemingly impossible prophecy. Ezekiel 37:1-10 reads like this, "*The LORD took hold of me, and I was carried away by the Spirit of the LORD to a valley filled with bones. He led me all around among the bones that covered the valley floor. They were scattered everywhere across the ground and were completely dried out.*

Then He asked me, 'Son of man, can these bones become living people again?' 'O Sovereign LORD,' I replied, 'you alone know the answer to that.' Then he said to me, 'Speak a prophetic message to these bones and say, Dry bones, listen to the word of the LORD! This is what the Sovereign LORD says: Look! I am going to put breath into you and make you live again! I will put flesh and muscles on you and cover you with skin. I will put breath into you, and you will come to life. **Then you will know**

> Isaiah 11:12, "*He will raise a flag among the nations and assemble the exiles of Israel. He will gather the scattered people of Judah from the ends of the earth.*"

that I am the LORD.' *So, I spoke this message, just as He told me.*

Suddenly as I spoke, there was a rattling noise all across the valley. The bones of each body came together and attached themselves as complete skeletons. Then as I watched, muscles and flesh formed over the bones. Then skin formed to cover their bodies, but they still had no breath in them.

Then He said to me, 'Speak a prophetic message to the winds, son of man. Speak a prophetic message and say, this is what the Sovereign LORD says: Come, O breath, from the four winds! Breathe into these dead bodies so they may live again.' So, I spoke the message as He commanded me, and breath came into their bodies. They all came to life and stood up on their feet—a great army."

God then explained to Ezekiel what he had just witnessed. The prophecy is nothing short of breathtaking considering its recent fulfillment, as we are about to see. Ezekiel 37:11-12 says, "*Then He said to me, 'Son of man, these bones represent the people of Israel. They are saying,* **'We have become old, dry bones—all hope is gone. Our nation is finished.'** *Therefore, prophesy to them and say, 'This is what the Sovereign LORD says: O my people,* **I will open your graves of exile and cause you to rise again. Then I will bring you back to the land of Israel.'**"

God distinctly said that when the Jews were at their absolute lowest, without hope, completely ruined, and most desperate, He would take them out of exile and return them to Israel.

Prophecy Fulfilled. When were the Jews at their absolute lowest, without hope, completely ruined, and most desperate? For sure it was when they were on the verge of extinction with no hope at all, during World War II, when a demon possessed despot was vilely obsessed with killing the very last Jew in the world. Jews were on the brink of complete annihilation after nearly all the Jews in Europe had been killed. In fact, practically half of all Jews in the world were killed during the short period of WWII.

A few years later, God chose to return them to their own reborn country of Israel on May 14th, 1948, after nearly 2,000 years of exile among the nations of the world. This was only three years after near extermination in the ovens and gas chambers of Auschwitz and the other concentration camps of the Nazi regime.

This is truly a most incredible fulfillment of prophecy. The Jewish people survived 2,000 years of dispersal, fragmentation, subjugation, abuse, and holocaust and still returned to their country intact with their culture, language, and religion. To fully appreciate this, consider the account of the Taino Indians of the Caribbean:

> *God chose to return the Jews to their own reborn country of Israel on May 14th, 1948, just 3 years after the ovens of Auschwitz.*

When Christopher Columbus landed in the Caribbean in 1492, the Taino people lived on the present-day islands of Cuba, Puerto Rico, Haiti, Hispaniola, Jamaica, and the Bahamas. In less than 100 years their language, religion and culture were gone, and the Spanish government declared them extinct, although traces of their DNA still exist in the Caribbean.

This huge ethnic group disappeared in 100 years while the Jews miraculously survived two millennia with their religion, culture, and language intact. They survived in spite of perennial prejudice against them, dispersal throughout the whole earth, and multiple organized genocides including the Nazi death camps.

In closing this topic, I should mention that not until 2023 were more Jews in Israel than were elsewhere. So, most Jews are now in Israel. The prophecies indicate, however, that virtually all Jews will one day return to Israel.

Most Jews not in Israel, today, are in the United States. Since the re-establishment of the nation of Israel in 1948, and before, persecution of the Jews has been the driving force to motivate their return to Israel from the countries of the world.

What will be the result of the shameless and barefaced hatred for the Jews we are seeing today in the United States and abroad? The October 2023 massacre of over 1,500 Jews by Hamas terrorists exposed heinous acts against women and children—carnage that included cruel beheadings of live human beings with garden hoes. (I saw the videos but had to look away as the hoe blade came down on the live victim's neck.) Not even babies were exempted from beheadings.

Yet, we have seen mass demonstrations everywhere, including the U.S., in support of these monstrous horrors. Accompanying these antisemitic demonstrations there has been a 337% increase in hate crimes against Jewish people, according to the Anti-Defamation League that monitors such things. This will doubtlessly induce more Jewish emigration back to Israel, just as the prophecies foretold.

But, more than that, in view of these anti-Semitic demonstrations, we cannot deny the scary truth that the abhorrent and bestial people that ran the Nazi death camps live all around us, still, today. It is the same mentality. It is the same spirit. It is a satanic hatred for the Jews, apparent throughout history, where no brutality is too extreme, and no ghoulish atrocity fails to delight them.

Who is not aware that when the presidents of three of the most prestigious universities in America (Penn State, MIT and Harvard) were giving testimony before the US Congress, not a single one would answer "Yes" to this question posed by New York congresswoman Elise Stefanick in December of 2023: *"At [university name], does the calling for the genocide of Jews violate [university name] rules of bullying and harassment?"*

If our most prestigious universities represent the pinnacle of our civilization, then as a nation we are "dead men walking." For this is where tomorrow's leaders were taught to hate and to ignore any vestige of basic human decency as they proudly parade their moral depravity with no shame at all. For what is more perverse than a bloodthirsty and frenzied mob rabidly demanding genocide?

Without the most primordial moral instincts, instead of repudiating unspeakable barbarity, they defend it—even encourage it.

Who would have guessed that 2023 would see a return to the mass murder of Jewish mothers and fathers and children, at the applause of much of the world? We thought that the Holocaust was civilization's shameful failure of *last* century. But here we are repeating it again.

Welcome to your world, today. This is no time to be without the eternal security and moral certitude that can only be found in Jesus, when all around us is a dangerous and alarming refusal to call such vicious savagery, evil.

If not in Jesus, then where is the world to find a moral tether in the face of rapidly increasing unrestrained hatred, today? Especially when higher education, historically believed to be a mooring of civilization, has been exposed to be promoting racism, hatred and genocide.

Return to Never Leave Again

Let me share another little prophecy that everyone ought to know. It is actually an ongoing prophecy that continues to be fulfilled. Be aware that God said that once the Jews returned to Israel, they would never be uprooted from their homeland again.

The prophecy is found in Amos 9:15 and says, "'*I will plant them on their land, and they shall **never again be uprooted out of the land** that I have given them,' says the LORD your God.*"

Notice the assertive, almost cocky way God says the same thing in Jeremiah 31: 35 & 36, "*This is what the LORD says, he who appoints the sun to shine by day, who decrees the moon and stars to shine by night, who stirs up the sea so that its waves roar — the LORD Almighty is his name: 'Only if these decrees vanish from my sight,' declares the LORD, 'will the descendants of Israel ever cease to be a nation before me.'*"

If I did not believe the Bible, I would have to question this prophecy. Due to the overwhelming and escalating hatred for the Jews, one must come to the conclusion that eventually, the world will have its way with them, and they will be no more. The United States' support for Israel has been significant, though not always stalwart, in recent years. However, there are strong and growing political winds in the US that are pushing our government to join the rest of the world in their contempt for the Jews.

If I were a betting man who did not trust the Bible, I would have to conclude that the Jews' days are numbered. In fact, the Bible tells us that they would, indeed, one day be crushed if Jesus delayed His return. Jesus will save them, though, when they are again on the very verge of final annihilation.

> *Amos 9:15*
> *"'I will plant them on their land, and they shall never again be uprooted out of the land that I have given them,' says the LORD your God."*

There has been an unsuccessful, but non-stop effort to chase the Jews from Israel since 1948. As a matter of fact, in just the short time since the rebirth of Israel, they have already had nine wars and two Palestinian intifadas in addition to a whole series of armed conflicts; not to mention the constant threat of missile bombardment, suicide bombings, and public place knifings. Yet God's promise still stands.

Two Nations to Become One

Now for an example of Biblical clarity...
Notice with what explicitness and detail God foretold that when the Jews returned to Israel they would return as one nation and not as two. Remember, after just the third king of Israel, the country had a revolution and was divided into the two nations of Israel in the north and Judah in the south.

Just as it had been prophesied, the northern kingdom of Israel was the first to go into Assyrian captivity in 722 BC because of their idolatry. During the entire 209-year history of the northern kingdom, it did not have a single king who honored the true God who performed all those miracles to bring them out of Egypt and into their promised homeland.

The southern kingdom of Judah, though likewise idolatrous, did have a smattering of good kings respectful of God. Consequently, they lasted a bit longer, but finally, as foretold, they too succumbed to the consequences of their rebellion against God, and went into captivity in Babylon 136 years later, in 586 BC.

As is the case with most Bible prophecies, this one was also declared multiple times from multiple sources spanning hundreds of years. Hosea 1:11 is one account of this prophecy. It reads, *"The people of Judah and the people of Israel will be reunited, and they will appoint one leader..."*

Nearly 200 years later, this is how the prophecy of their eventual return to Israel, as one nation, reads in Ezekiel 37:21-22, *"I will gather the people of Israel from among the nations. I will bring them home to their own land from the places where they have been scattered. I will **unify them into one nation** on the mountains of Israel. **One king will rule them all; no longer will they be divided into two nations or into two kingdoms.**"*

Prophecy Fulfilled. First, God says He will *unite them into one nation*. Then, in case that was too ambiguous for somebody, He repeats Himself by saying that *only one king would rule over them*. Finally, in case someone still wasn't listening, He repeats Himself a third time by saying that the Jews would *no longer be divided into two nations or two kingdoms*. Any questions?

> Ezekiel 37:22
> I will unify them into one nation on the mountains of Israel. One king will rule them all; no longer will they be divided into two nations or into two kingdoms."

In perfect accordance with the prophecy, the single nation of Israel today includes both the ancient areas of the northern kingdom of Israel and the southern kingdom of Judah.

Notice, unlike Nostradamus' quatrains, this is not a prophecy that anyone must wait until after its fulfillment to understand. You cannot miss the clarity, the detail, and the repetition.

Israel to be Formed in One Day

Speak of clarity and detail! God foretold that the new Jewish nation of Israel would be formed in a single day. What unusual minutiae to include! You can see God's attention to detail in an attempt to build our confidence in His word.

Look at what He says in Isaiah 66:8, *"Who has ever seen anything as strange as this? Who ever heard of such a thing? Has a nation ever been **born in a single day**? Has a **country ever come forth in a mere moment**? But by the time Jerusalem's birth pains begin, her children will be born."*

Prophecy Fulfilled. As you know, Israel became a nation on May 14th, 1948, without a shot being fired. I mention, *without a shot being fired*, because there is more to the story that we will see in a moment. This verse likens the rebirth of the nation of Israel to the birth of a baby. Notice, that this verse says that the nation will be *"born in a single day,"* and that before the labor pains really start, the birth is over. That is exactly what happened when the nation was born in a single day without the birth pains of a war for independence.

However, we need to look at the previous verse to this one in order to get the whole story.

War for independence to occur AFTER the country is formed.

Whoever heard of a war for independence being fought AFTER the country has already been formally recognized by the world? What country was ever formed *before* their war for independence was fought? But let's see what Isaiah 66:7 says. *"Before she was in labor she gave birth;* **before her pain came** *upon her she delivered a son."* And remember, we know this speaks of the rebirth of Israel because the very next verse that we previously read says, *"Has a nation ever been born in a single day? Has a country ever come forth in a mere moment?"*

Prophecy Fulfilled. *"...before her pain came upon her, she delivered a son."* So, there WAS pain, but not until AFTER the birth. That is exactly what happened when the day after Israel was formed, Iraq, Lebanon, Transjordan, Syria, and Egypt simultaneously attacked this baby nation.

Israel's labor pains were felt AFTER the birth of the country, just like the prophecy from over 2,500 years earlier predicted.

By the way, any betting person would have had to put their money on the five-nation coalition that attacked the newborn baby state. That person, however, would have lost the bet, since that was a God-thing going on there. Books have been written about the miracles which occurred during that war. Those miracles saved this tiny country, of less than one million citizens, from annihilation by the five surrounding nations with a total population of around 30 million at that time. That's right, less than one million against thirty million!

Israel Would Include Jerusalem

Here is another detail which God was explicit about. He said that when He brought the Jews back to Israel, it would include the city of Jerusalem. That may seem unremarkable, but wait until you hear the whole story.

You see, following the war for independence in 1948, there was the Armistice Agreement of 1949 between Israel and the five nations that had attacked her. The armistice was supervised by the United Nations.

According to this arrangement, while Israeli territory included some of the newer parts of the city of Jerusalem, it included none of the old walled city or the Temple Mount—the part of the city that was most precious to the new nation of Israel.

For Israel, the Armistice Agreement of 1949 was bitter-sweet and a little like a kiss without a hug. And there was absolutely no hope of concession from Jordan, which controlled the old walled city of Jerusalem and the Temple Mount.

But the Jews still had God's prophetic promise that they would one day control Jerusalem. True Christian believers stood with them, pointing to the prophecies in the Bible, like Zechariah 8:4-8 which says, "*Once again* **old men and women will walk Jerusalem's streets** *with their canes and will sit together in the city squares. And* **the streets of the city will be filled with boys and girls at play**. *This is what the LORD of*

Heaven's Armies says: All this may seem impossible to you now, a small remnant of God's people. But is it impossible for me? says the LORD of Heaven's Armies. This is what the LORD of Heaven's Armies says: You can be sure that I will rescue My people from the east and from the west. **I will bring them home again to live safely in Jerusalem.**"

Needless to say, no one but true believers thought it possible that the Jews would ever control the old city of Jerusalem again. All others were thinking that these silly Jews and Christians had no sense of the realities of international politics.

Prophecy Fulfilled. You probably know that today Israel includes all of the old walled city of Jerusalem, as well as the Temple Mount. (Note: In an attempt to promote peace with the Muslim population in the country, Israel has relinquished management of the Temple Mount to the Islamic wakf.)

What happened to make an impossibility a reality? The Six Day War of 1967 happened.

Here's how it all started. The southern tip of Israel and the port city of Eilat, are on the northern tip of the Gulf of Aqaba. The southern end of the Gulf of Aqaba opens into the Red Sea through the Straits of Tiran. From there, the southern end of the Red Sea provides access to Africa and all points east including India, China, and the Pacific Ocean. From the northern end of the Red Sea there is access to the Mediterranean Sea, Europe, and the Atlantic Ocean.

Notes:
1. Israel pre-1967 borders—white area only
2. Grey areas were acquired in the Six Day War
3. Tiny Gaza Strip given to Palestinian National Authority in 1993. Hamas now dominates.
4. Sinai returned to Egypt in 1982

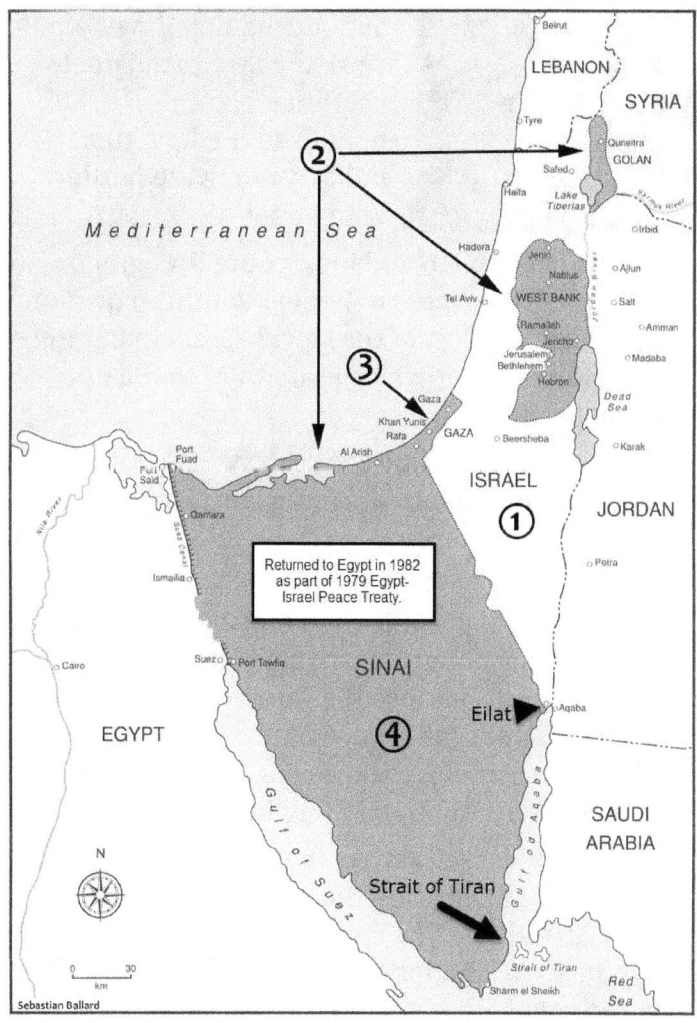

Here is the problem. Egypt controlled the huge Sinai Peninsula and the tiny Straits of Tiran at the southern tip of the peninsula—the entry point into the Red Sea. (See map previous page.)

In May of 1967, Egypt threw out the United Nations Emergency Force that supervised activity at the Straits of Tiran and announced that Egypt would close the Straits to Israeli shipping. They also mobilized the Egyptian military along the border with Israel.

> *What happened to make an impossibility a reality?*
>
> *The Six Day War of 1967 happened.*

This was in violation of the UN agreement and cut off all access to Israel's southern port of Eilat from the rest of the world. Israel found this egregious and unfair and said they would not stand for it.

The battle lines were drawn. Egypt, though, had military alliances with Israel's other neighbors, Jordan and Syria. Israel was alone and surrounded again.

Israel's enemies had 600 aircraft—the Israelis, only about 200. Israel had only French made aircraft because the American president, Lyndon Baines Johnson, would not sell them any US planes. Israel's enemies' air forces included sophisticated Russian MiG fighter jets.

The Israelis knew they were at a huge disadvantage. In 1967 the population of Israel was only 2.5 million. The combined population of Egypt, Syria, and Jordan was over 35 million. Did you get that—2.5 million against 35 million? They knew that they would somehow have to achieve air superiority to even have a chance.

Every morning, for the previous two years, Egyptian, Jordanian, and Syrian radar monitors would watch as Israeli fighters would take off over the Mediterranean, then drop off the radar as they plunged to a low flying altitude to return home. June 5th, 1967 at 7:15 a.m. was no different, except that this time 183 planes, nearly the entire Israeli Airforce, took off. As always, they dropped from radar as they flew at just 60 feet above the water. But this time, instead of returning home, they turned south and showed up, completely unexpected, over the Egyptian airfields.

This brilliant maneuver gave the Israelis air superiority when they were successful in destroying the entire Egyptian Airforce. This gave Israel at least a fighting chance in the war they were about to have on three fronts, simultaneously, with three separate larger countries.

Doubtlessly God was with them when they won the war in six days. While the Israeli Defense Force lost less than 1,000 troops, their enemies lost 20,000. While the IDF lost only a handful of planes, their enemies lost nearly all of theirs.

As a result of the war, Israel ended up in possession of the entire Sinai Peninsula and Gaza Strip from Egypt, the West Bank from Jordan, and the Golan Heights from Syria. These were all highly strategic areas.

> *June 5th, 1967 at 7:15 a.m. was no different, except that this time 183 planes, nearly the entire Israeli Airforce, took off.*

Before Israel acquired the area of the West Bank from Jordan, the middle of Israel was less than 9 miles wide. Before winning the Golan Heights from Syria, Syrian tanks would harass the Israeli farmers below. Before winning the Sinai Peninsula from Egypt, Israel was at the mercy of Egypt to allow them through the Strait of Tiran.

But the greatest inspiration for this newly reborn nation came with the ultimate prize—the entire old walled city of Jerusalem and the precious Temple Mount.

Today, old Jewish men and women do indeed walk with their canes on the streets of the old city of Jerusalem while Jewish children play there, exactly as the prophecies said they would. I have seen, for myself, that it is true.

Jerusalem: A Political Problem

Inspired by God to prophesy, Zechariah foretold that the city of Jerusalem would be a political problem for the world at this time in history. Now, you might say, "duh", because it is so obviously true; but remember that the prophecy was made 2,500 years ago.

Twenty-five hundred years ago Jerusalem was a destroyed, worthless, and miserable fringe city of the vast Persian Empire. Jerusalem's past greatness had become only a distant memory.

To expect that it would ever again take center stage in world politics, as it has today, was crazy talk at that time. You can read Zechariah 12:2-3 for yourself, "*Behold, I will make **Jerusalem a cup of trembling** unto all the people round about...and in that day will I make **Jerusalem a burdensome stone for all people**: all that burden themselves with it shall be cut in pieces, though all the people of the earth are gathered together against it.*"

Prophecy Being Fulfilled. This prophecy will be completed over time, but we can already see its partial fulfillment. Who does not know that Jerusalem is at the center of world politics right now? Who does not know that anyone who has ever tried to solve its problems has only found it to be a *heavy, burdensome stone*? Just ask Presidents

> *As bad as the problems are that surround Jerusalem right now, the worst is yet to come. But so is the best!*

Nixon, Ford, Carter, Reagan, G.H.W. Bush, Clinton, G.W. Bush, Obama, Trump and Biden.

If you read the prophecy carefully, you will get a glimpse into the future of Israel. You might notice that as bad as the problems are that surround Jerusalem right now, the worst is yet to come. But so is the best!

Israel Renowned For Its Agriculture

When most people think of Israel, they picture desert, dust, donkeys, and camels. While that would be an accurate description of Israel before 1948, things have changed since then.

To appreciate the agricultural wonder that is Israel today, one must understand what it was like before the Jews returned in 1948. Mark Twain visited the land in 1867. Here are his comments as expressed in his book "The Innocents Abroad," published in 1869:

"Palestine sits in sackcloth and ashes. Over it broods the spell of a curse that has withered its fields and fettered its energies... Jericho the accursed, lies a moldering ruin, today, even as Joshua's miracle left it more than three thousand year ago; Bethlehem and Bethany, in their poverty and their humiliation, have nothing about them now to remind one that they once knew the high honor of the Savior's presence... **Renowned Jerusalem itself, the stateliest name in history, has lost all its ancient grandeur, and is become a pauper village.**"

Mark Twain's statement contributes to the fulfillment of another prophecy declared in Jeremiah 22:8 and elsewhere. "People from many nations will pass by this city and will ask one another, `Why has the LORD done such a thing to this great city?'" And in Ezekiel 5:14 God says it this way, "*I will make you a desolation and a disgrace among the nations which surround you and in the sight of all who pass by."*

However, God was clear that once the Jewish nation was reborn, it would become a breadbasket—because He would make it one. We find the prophecy, among other places, in Ezekiel 34:29 which says, *"And I will make their land **famous for its crops**, so my people will never again suffer from famines or the insults of foreign nations."*

The prophecy was made multiple times. Here it is, again, in Isaiah 27:6. *"The time is coming when Jacob's descendants will take root. **Israel will bud and blossom and fill the whole earth with fruit!**"*

Prophecy Fulfilled. Anyone who goes to Israel today, will be struck by the stunning abundance and variety of its agriculture. The view of fertile fields you see when flying into Tel Aviv's Ben Gurion Airport is hardly even a hint of the cornucopia that is Israeli produce. It is indeed sold around the world; though it must often be repackaged in other countries to avoid the discrimination that exists against their produce and merchandise. It must be so because of worldwide bigotry against them.

> *The view of fertile fields you see when flying into Tel Aviv's Ben Gurion Airport is only a hint of the cornucopia of Israeli produce.*

The agricultural discoveries, inventions, and innovations of the tiny nation of Israel impact, in no small way, the entire world. It would take volumes and volumes to do justice to the subject of

Israeli agricultural advancements; however, unless you are a horticulturist or botanist you would probably find it boring.

Allow me, though, to at least list for you 12 of the more popular fruits and vegetables developed in Israel in very recent years, but grown and consumed the world over. The list would include the Galia melon, Orangetti spaghetti squash, Nectarine-mango, Pomelit grapefruit-pomelo, seedless bell pepper, Black Galaxy tomato, Goldy zucchini squash, Nano Watermelon, mini basil tree, TableSugar acorn squash, cluster (Truss) tomatoes, and the Anna apple. There are special qualities about each of these fruits and vegetables that make them superior to their variety siblings.

Israeli agricultural technology is highly sought after, and they generously share with the world the amazing advancements in agronomy that have been invented and discovered there.

Israeli innovation encompasses every area of agricultural in every region of this small country, including the incredibly harsh deserts of the Negev and Arabah valley in the south.

One example of Israeli innovation would be the jojoba farms of the Negev desert. The jojoba plant produces an oil used predominantly in cosmetics because of its similarity to the natural oil of human skin. The jojoba plant was introduced to Israel only 30 years ago and already Israel has captured a full 50% of the entire jojoba worldwide market.

One of the largest fish farms in the world is in the Arabah valley of the Negev desert—a place that receives less than two inches of rain per year.

In this isolated and severe desert environment you will also find prawn farms. Prawns, though scientifically different, are almost indistinguishable from shrimp. I mention these prawn farms to highlight the amazing and revolutionary research occurring all over Israel from medicine to technology to farming to prawns. Israeli research discovered an agent that will block the gene that creates the hormone for male organs in these prawns.

> *The jojoba plant was introduced to Israel only 30 years ago and already Israel has captured a full 50% of the entire jojoba worldwide market.*

At this remote desert prawn farm, who would imagine that they are injecting baby male prawns, smaller than a grain of rice, with this agent? After silencing the male organ hormone, these male prawns grow female organs and mate with other male prawns producing much, much larger prawns.

You might not know that the market in China, Vietnam and Southeast Asia is huge for these unique prawns. Israel exports over 400,000 tons every year. That is nearly a billion pounds of prawns.

Israeli research also curiously discovered that these prawn hybrids are voracious predators of an African fresh-water snail that causes a horribly disfiguring disease that kills 200,000 people a year and infects another 200 million more. The plan is to use these unique male prawns as biocontrol agents to eliminate this disease. This is one more way that Israel is a blessing to those beyond her borders.

In 1979, Israel's agriculture accounted for about 6% of GDP as well as a healthy percentage of its exports. Despite tremendous growth in agriculture during the ensuing years, today it represents a smaller percentage of GDP and exports. That is because of the enormous expansion in Israeli technology and R&D, which is second only to Silicon Valley. All other areas of the Israeli economy, from medicine to the petroleum industry, have likewise seen the massive expansion that agriculture has—just like the prophecy said it would.

Israel to be Militarily Formidable

As we previously noted, God promised that once the Jews returned to Israel they would never be routed again. So far this has held true. Since the book that tells the future promises this, I expect it to be so going forward as well. We do know, though, that Israel will one day be invaded and nearly crushed, but not ultimately conquered, because Jesus will not let that happen when He steps in at the last moment. In the meantime…

The Bible foretold over 2,500 years ago that Israel would have a strong military in the last days. Zechariah 12:6 says, *"On that day I will make the clans of Judah like a flame that sets a woodpile ablaze or like a burning torch among sheaves of grain. They will burn up all the neighboring nations right and left, while the people living in Jerusalem remain secure."* While we have certainly seen partial fulfillment of this prophecy, maybe we have not seen its ULTIMATE fulfillment, since we expect that there is more to come.

Israel a nuclear power

There will be more wars in the Middle East that involve Israel. This verse and others make that clear, but we know what the outcomes will be. Though Israel, indeed, has a powerful military, it still ranks behind both Iran and Egypt in conventional weaponry. But conventional weaponry is not everything.

Never forget that Israel is a nuclear power, and so far, none of its neighbors are. In fact, there are only nine nations with nuclear capability in the world today. Israel is one of them. The nations are: the US, the UK, Russia, France, China, India, Pakistan, North Korea, and Israel.

Little country, big fist

In terms of land mass, Israel ranks 149th in the countries of the world—10% smaller than even Belize. In terms of population it ranks 97th—5% smaller than even the United Arab Emirates. Yet in terms of its military might, it is currently ranked at 18th in the world, ahead of Taiwan, Spain and Poland. While it is remarkable that this tiny country has such a formidable military and is ranked as the 18th most powerful nation without even counting its nuclear status, you must remember that it wouldn't really matter if Israel was ranked dead last, because God…

> *It wouldn't really matter if Israel was ranked last in military might, because God…*

The Mossad

The Israeli intelligence service, Mossad, is second to none in the world. The incredible successes they have enjoyed in the short life of the nation are most impressive. Their many achievements include the precision military assault on the terrorist-controlled airport of Entebbe, Uganda in 1976 which freed an entire airplane load of hostages and inspired several movies.

In 1960, the Mossad found the Nazi henchman and mastermind of Germany's genocide of Europe's Jews, Adolf Eichmann. He was living comfortably in Argentina under the assumed name of Ricardo Klement. Mossad agents covertly kidnapped him and smuggled him out of the country for trial and execution in Israel.

Then there was 9/11. Wikipedia describes Mossad's involvement this way in the article *https://en.wikipedia.org/wiki/Mossad*, *"Mossad informed the FBI and CIA in August 2001 that, based on its intelligence, as many as 200 terrorists were slipping into the United States and planning a 'major assault on the United States.' The Israeli intelligence agency cautioned the FBI that it had picked up indications of a 'large-scale target' in the United States and that Americans would be 'very vulnerable.'"*

We all know what happened next.

Israeli Military Related Statistics

For your curiosity I will share some June 2020 military statistics from *worldometers.info*:

Total population: 8,424,904

Total military personnel: 615,000 (estimated)

Total aircraft strength: 595 (ranked 18th out of 137)

Fighter aircraft: 253 (ranked 11th)

Combat tanks: 2,760 (ranked 8th)

Total naval assets: 65

Defense budget: $20 billion

Top 15 World Military Budget Rankings

(per https://en.wikipedia.org/wiki/List_of_countries_by_military_expenditures#External_links)

Rank	Country	Spending (US$ bn)
1	United States	738.0
2	China	193.3
3	India	64.1
4	United Kingdom	61.5
5	Russia	60.6
6	France	56.8
7	Germany	51.3
8	Japan	49.7
9	Saudi Arabia	48.5
10	South Korea	40.4
11	Australia	31.3
12	Italy	29.3
13	Brazil	22.1
14	Canada	20.0
15	Israel	19.9

Curse on Chorazin, Bethsaida, and Capernaum

Even the minor details in the Bible are accurate. Jesus visited the towns of Chorazin, Bethsaida, and Capernaum, but did few miracles there because of the people's lack of faith.

Because of their unbelief, it was disheartening for Him that He could not bless them as He desired. You can sense His strong frustration when He made this proclamation in Matthew 11:21-24, *"Woe to you, **Chorazin**! Woe to you, **Bethsaida**! For if the miracles that were performed in you had been performed in Tyre and Sidon, they would have repented long ago in sackcloth and ashes. But I tell you, it will be more bearable for Tyre and Sidon on the day of judgment than for you.*

*And you, **Capernaum**, will you be lifted to the heavens? No, you will go down to Hades. For if the miracles that were performed in you had been performed in Sodom, it would have remained to this day. But I tell you that it will be more bearable for Sodom on the day of judgment than for you."*

Jesus plainly warned these three cities that when the time came to answer to God, it would not go well for them. Jesus shamed the Jewish cities of Chorazin and Bethsaida by contrasting them with the pagan cities of Tyre and Sidon. He told them that the pagans of Tyre and Sidon, had He gone there, would have responded better to God's truth than these Jewish cities had.

The Jews had the Scriptures and were supposed to be the enlightened ones. Jesus continued by saying that eternal judgement would be harsher for these Jewish cities than for the pagan cities because the Jews had received a more clear presentation of the truth.

Then Jesus really unloaded on Capernaum, telling that city that Sodom's eternal punishment (you remember what happened to Sodom and Gomorrah in Genesis 19) would be less severe than Capernaum's, because Capernaum had so blatantly rejected the truth.

This is an important fact to note. Those who have heard and rejected a clear presentation of God's truth will be judged much more severely. The book that tells the future is replete with this warning.

Prophecy Fulfilled. Jesus pronounced a curse on these three cities when He said, "Woe to you..." These three cities were at the north end of the beautiful Sea of Galilee. Capernaum was a charming location right on the shore. These would be great locations for cities or towns today, but none of them have been rebuilt. I've been there and have seen the ruins for myself.

> Those who have heard and rejected a clear presentation of God's truth will be judged much more severely. So says the book that tells the future.

Except for the fact that Jesus said, "Woe to you..." about Chorazin, Bethsaida, and Capernaum, there seems to be no reason why they should not be thriving communities today. Interestingly, they are not.

What's the Big Deal with the Jews?

We have considered many currently fulfilling Bible prophecies concerning Israel and the Jews. Now, would probably be a good time to answer an important question that a curious mind might be thinking.

"Why do we see God's promises, blessings, and faithfulness to the Jewish people when, for the most part, they will not admit who Jesus was? Why would God center the prophecies of end time events around a people group who, generally speaking, up to now, have rejected their own Messiah?"

As background for the answer to that question, it would be informative to first consider how the Jews find themselves in their current spiritual condition. Volumes could be written on this subject; but in the simplest terms, the Jews were expecting their messiah to be a mighty deliverer from the Roman oppression that they suffered under at the time of Christ. They weren't expecting a humble messiah that would deliver them from the consequences of sin, even though many Old Testament scriptures, including Isaiah 53, described Him in specific detail.

The horrible mistake of rejecting the Messiah set them on a sad and dark path. History makes that undeniably obvious. But as the prophecies you'll read in the next chapters show, God still has a plan for the Jewish people that is in full swing right now.

The Messiah will indeed come as a mighty deliverer the next time, when Israel is about to be crushed, as described in Ezekiel 38 & 39. However, He came as a humble deliverer of men's souls the first time, just as hundreds of Old Testament prophecies predicted.

I want to share with you one of these amazing prophecies found in Daniel 9. We will look at verse 25 which says, "Seven sets of seven plus sixty-two sets of seven will pass from the time the command is given to rebuild Jerusalem until a ruler—the Anointed One—comes."

> *The horrible mistake of rejecting the Messiah set them on a sad and dark path. History makes that undeniably obvious.*

The prophecy says that 7 X 7(49) plus 62 X 7 (434) (for a total of 483) years would pass from the time the decree was given to rebuild Jerusalem until the Anointed One would come.

It turns out that Artaxerxes made several decrees allowing the Jews to return to Jerusalem from Persia. The first decree occurred in his 7th year. 483 years are calculated by some to end on the day John the Baptist said this about Jesus in John 1:29, "*Behold, the Lamb of God, who takes away the sin of the world,*" fulfilling the prophecy. (See: *www.5loaves2fishes.net/artaxerxes-decree*)

However, Artaxerxes' second decree was made in his 20th year. 483 years from that time is carefully calculated by others to bring you to Palm Sunday, 33 A.D. (See: *biblical-thinking.org/cgi-bin/article.pl?314*)

We all know who rode a donkey on that day through the Golden Gate on the eastern side of the Temple Mount as the people cried, *"Hosanna to the son of David: Blessed is He that cometh in the name of the Lord; Hosanna in the highest".*

Who else could this prophecy possibly be talking about? If not Jesus, then who? History points to no other figure—an Anointed One who would "atone for iniquity"—who could fulfill this astonishing Old Testament prophecy at that time—or ever! After all, no one can "atone for iniquity," but God himself.

As if that wasn't enough, the Old Testament prophecy in Daniel 9 goes on to say in verse 26 that this would all happen before the second temple was destroyed, which history records occurred in 70 A.D. Furthermore, the same verse says, *"the anointed one shall be cut off."* Who doesn't know how Jesus' life was cut short at the cross?

By the way, every true believer knows that the Jews did not kill Jesus. You and I did. Actually, we all did. He intentionally laid His life down in order to pay the eternal consequences of humanity's sin, offering mankind the possibility of not having to pay those consequences themselves.

Jesus was the unblemished human sacrifice that all the Old Testament Jewish animal sacrifices anticipated. And it was our sin that made it necessary that God, being the only innocent, would have to pay the penalty for our sin on the cross.

What's up with all the animal sacrifices?

Many societies throughout history have sacrificed animals to appease demon gods. Muslims, also, celebrate animal sacrifice during their yearly "Festival of Sacrifice." They say, per the Quran, that it is to honor Abraham's willingness to slay his son Ishmael at Allah's request. (see As-Safat 37:102-107) This was not compiled until 644-656 CE, shortly after Mohammad's death in 632 CE, and sounds vaguely similar to the Biblical account written over 2,000 years earlier.

The Biblical account, however, tells a much different story and explains animal sacrifice for a much different reason than every other animal-sacrificing religion. The animal sacrifices of the Old Testament, which symbolized atonement for sin, were a picture of the real atonement for sin that would come when a perfect person, God Himself in the person of Jesus Christ, would choose to be that ultimate sacrifice—not simply *symbolizing* the atonement for sin, but rather becoming *the actual atonement* for all sin for all time. Such a beautiful, perfect, and clear picture we see of Jesus' crucifixion in all those Old Testament sacrifices.

> *The Old Testament animal sacrifices were a picture of the real atonement that would come when the perfect human sacrifice — Jesus—would truly atone for all sin.*

Jesus in the Old Testament?

There are numerous references to Jesus in the Old Testament, like Psalm 22 that mentions His rejection, pierced hands and feet, and the soldiers' gambling for His garments. But let's look at Isaiah 53. Although the entire chapter points to Jesus in amazing detail, we will consider verses 3-6 that read, *"He was despised and rejected by men, a man of sorrows and acquainted with grief; and as one from whom men hide their faces he was despised, and we esteemed him not. Surely, he has borne our griefs and carried our sorrows; yet we esteemed him stricken, smitten by God, and afflicted. But he was **pierced for our transgressions**; he was **crushed for our iniquities**; **upon him was the chastisement that brought us peace**, and with his wounds we are healed. All we like sheep have gone astray; we have turned everyone to his own way; and **the LORD has laid on him the iniquity of us all**."*

These, and so many other Old Testament scriptures like them, clearly describe Jesus and His ultimate sacrifice for man's sin. All the Old Testament sacrifices point to Him and what He did at the cross. Jesus is now looking for those who would simply love Him back for the supreme demonstration of love that was evidenced at the cross by His death. Is that too much to ask?

I should mention that Isaiah 53 is considered a "forbidden chapter" in many synagogues. Though commonly ignored, the honest person will remember that it was, of course, included in the Isaiah scroll found among the Dead Sea Scrolls at Qumran, dating from 200 years before Christ. This is the oldest copy of Isaiah that exists today. You can find the most amazing information about "the forbidden chapter" on *YouTube* in these videos:

https://www.youtube.com/watch?v=cGz9BVJ_k6s
https://www.youtube.com/watch?v=XB4hexLWCdc

Many, many other specific Old Testament prophecies make the possibility of the Jewish Messiah being anyone other than Jesus, a statistical impossibility. The prophecies say He would be born in Bethlehem, would travel to Egypt, would be a descendent of Abraham, Isaac, and Jacob, would be rejected by His own people, would be a Nazarene, would speak in parables, would be betrayed, would be crucified, and that He would be revealed BEFORE the destruction of the second temple, which occurred less than 40 years after His crucifixion and return to heaven.

All this was foretold in the Old Testament scriptures. And still Jewish eyes are blinded to these facts, just as the Scriptures also said they would be.

While it is only one of many such prophecies, I might also mention the prophecy of Jeremiah 31:15 that describes a massacre of children that would occur in Jesus' birthplace of Bethlehem. Matthew 2:16 describes what history also tells us—that this did indeed happen under King Herod the Great during the childhood of Jesus.

History shows us that all these prophecies were fulfilled in Jesus. After all, if God did not give us a clear description of the Messiah, how would we know who to look for? We might accept an imposter.

Israel's future is no mystery

Prophecies that describe the future of the Jewish nation are as plain, explicit, and obvious in Scripture as past Jewish history has been. What has happened, is currently happening, and will happen to the nation of Israel and the Jews has been no surprise and will continue to be no surprise to any real student of the Bible.

It truly boggles the mind that the Jewish nation remains blind to many of the Old Testament prophecies that describe what lies ahead for them, just like they have been temporarily blinded to the prophecies that point to Jesus in painful detail. It should really be no surprise, though, because Romans 11 predicted that it would be just as it is with regard to the Jewish nation's temporary oblivion. We will consider that prophecy in just a moment.

Back to the original question

Why is God concerned for the Jewish nation, considering that most of them reject Jesus and some of them are the greatest haters of God (leading atheist activists like Michael Newdow and Sam Harris) in the world? The answer is clear and unambiguous in Scripture. It is a prominent theme that runs throughout the entire Bible and is explained time and again in great detail. I will answer it with Scripture in three different ways.

First, God's care for the Jews is a result of His faithfulness to His promises to Abraham, Isaac, and Jacob, notwithstanding the Jewish nation's historic unfaithfulness to Him. God is clear that He would not break the promise that He made to their forefathers. Leviticus 26:44 says this, *"In spite of their unfaithfulness to me, I will not completely abandon them when they are dispersed throughout the world, because **I am the Lord their God and will not break my promises to them.**"*

Second, God says He will still be faithful to His promises to them even while they are in the act of rejecting Him. Despite the Jewish nation's unfaithfulness to God, He promises to remain faithful to them. Ezekiel 36:22 says this, *"Therefore say to the house of Israel, 'Thus says the Lord GOD: It is not for your sake, O house of Israel, that I am about to act, but for the sake of **my holy name, which you have profaned among the nations to which you came.**'"*

> *First, God's care for the Jews is a result of His faithfulness to His promises to Abraham, Isaac, and Jacob.*

Third, God has a plan. God knows that within His plan, the time will come when the entire Jewish nation will embrace Jesus, their Messiah. Romans 11:25-27, which I've already mentioned in part, says this to Christian Gentiles, *"I wouldn't want you to be ignorant of this great mystery, lest you get conceited; it's that the **Jews' rejection of Jesus is a temporary thing until the Gentiles' chance to know***

> *Second, God says He will still be faithful to His promises to Israel in spite of*

> *Third, God has a plan. God knows that within His plan, the time will come when the entire Jewish nation will embrace Jesus.*

God is completed. *Then, all Israel will be saved: as it is written in the Old Testament, 'There shall come out of Jerusalem the Deliverer, and shall **turn away ungodliness from Jacob**: For this is my covenant unto them, when **I shall take away their sins.**'*

The Romans passage above refers to chapter 59 and verse 20 of the Old Testament book of Isaiah. Zechariah also speaks of the time the Jews will finally embrace their Messiah and receive atonement (forgiveness of sins) from Him. Chapter 12, verse 10 describes it this way, *"And I will pour out on the Jews and the inhabitants of Jerusalem a spirit of grace and pleas for mercy, so that, **when they look on Me, on Him whom they have pierced, they shall mourn** for Him, as one mourns for an only child, **and weep bitterly** over Him, as one weeps over a firstborn."*

Zechariah 13:1 further describes their purification, *"In that day a fountain will be opened to the Jews and the inhabitants of Jerusalem, to cleanse them from sin and impurity."*

Verse 6 goes on to explain how the moment will go down when the scales fall from their eyes, and they recognize Jesus' nail-pierced hands and feet and His spear-pierced side. Notice what this clear Old Testament prophecy says, *"And if one asks him, 'What are these wounds on your body, he will say, 'The wounds I received in the house of my friends.'"*

You can only imagine the bitter remorse they will feel when they finally realize that they have been rejecting their own Messiah all along. God loves them so much and is continuing to be patient with them just as He has been patient with all of us.

I should point out that as the prophecy in Romans predicted, there are now hundreds of millions of Gentile followers of Yahweh (the Jewish name for God) who dearly love the Jews and are spiritual sons of Abraham. Real believers may be the only true friends that Israel has left.

These followers of Jesus are anxiously awaiting the fulfillment of prophecy concerning the day when the blinders will fall from the eyes of the Jewish nation, and they embrace their Messiah. I am more certain of this than I am certain that the moon is smaller than the sun. And why wouldn't I be? How irrational would I have to be to see the accuracy and impeccable sureness of Biblical prophecy up to this point and not have confidence in the next Bible prophecy?

Incidentally, here are some interesting verses in Hosea that describe God's discipline of the Jews and then their final deliverance, which will be both physical and spiritual. See Hosea 5:14-15 which says, *"For I will be like a lion to Ephraim, and like a young lion to the house of Judah. I, even I, will tear and go away; I will carry off, and no one shall rescue. I will return again to my place,* **until they acknowledge their guilt and seek my face***, and in their distress earnestly seek me."*

God has allowed punishment on the Jewish nation for their unfaithfulness to Him. You need not look beyond the Old Testament prophets or WWII to see that. The only part of this prophecy still waiting to be fulfilled is, *"...until they acknowledge their guilt and seek my face, and in their distress earnestly seek me."* This will happen. Just wait and see. Some might say, "Over my dead body." To which I would answer, "I truly hope not."

We see that God's interest in Israel and the Jewish people is, first, the result of His faithfulness to the promises He made to their forefathers. Secondly,

> God has future plans for the Jewish nation. God is not done with the Jews. He never was.

God also makes it clear that He will remain faithful to His promises in spite of the Jewish people's unfaithfulness to Him. And thirdly, God reveals that He has future plans for the Jewish nation. God is not done with the Jews. He never was.

If you find skepticism sneaking into your thinking, remind yourself that this all comes from the only book that tells the future. Remind yourself, also, who it is that most certainly does not want you to pay attention to such a book. Don't be deceived by his trickery.

Please be aware, too, that the Jews' rejection of Jesus is already beginning to soften as more and more Jews are coming to Jesus. Jews today, who follow Jesus, are commonly known as Messianic Jews. Before 1960 there was not a single Messianic Jewish congregation in all of Israel. Today, according to *https://en.wikipedia.org/wiki/Messianic_Judaism*, there are over a hundred Messianic Jewish congregations in Israel alone, with hundreds and hundreds more all over the world.

During our 2021 visit to Israel, we had a delightful Jewish woman for a guide. She was entertaining, and informative as she took us around to all the Old and New Testament sites in the country. Someone asked her how she could not be a Christian after being exposed to all the evidence that points to Jesus. She seemed internally conflicted as she explained what a scandal it would be for her large, close, and traditional Jewish family if she were to openly do so.

At this point in the Jewish story, their confirmation bias is just too strong for most of them to see the obvious. But we know the time is coming when that will all change. Meanwhile, true followers of Jesus will love them and stand with them against those who have only hatred for Israel and the Jews.

Prophecy Revealed in End Times

In the following chapters we will look at prophecies that don't specifically involve the Jews.

The Scriptures indicate that as we get closer and closer to the Lord's return, prophecy concerning the end times will be more fully revealed. God clearly declares that it is His intention to progressively reveal end time prophecy as we advance into that period. Scriptures like John 15:15, Amos 3:7, and others show us that it is God's desire to keep those informed who sincerely pursue a relationship with Him—who respect His word, the Bible.

Daniel was a devout man who certainly had God's ear because of his faithfulness to the Lord. In fact, angelic messengers that God sent to Daniel told him how esteemed he was by God. God shared many prophecies with Daniel through these angelic messengers. Some prophecies have already been fulfilled. We considered one of the past-fulfilled prophecies of Daniel in a previous chapter. Other prophecies of Daniel are being fulfilled right now and some have yet to be fulfilled.

There is one particular verse in Daniel that is overflowing with information about our day. Information, by the way, that Daniel would not see fulfilled in his time, but we are seeing fulfilled in ours. The verse is Daniel 12:4 which says, *"But you, Daniel, keep this prophecy a secret;* **seal up the book until the time of the end,** *when* **many**

will rush here and there, and ***knowledge will increase."***

Again, in verses 9 & 10 of the same chapter, when Daniel asks for an explanation of the prophecies revealed to him, this is the answer he receives, *"Go your way, Daniel, because* **the words are rolled up and sealed until the time of the end**. *Many will be purified, made spotless and refined, but the wicked will continue to be wicked. None of the wicked will understand,* **but those who are wise will understand**.*"*

> *Daniel 12:4*
> *"But you, Daniel, keep this prophecy a secret; seal up the book until the time of the end..."*

We clearly see that the prophecies will be revealed at *the time of the end*, and the "wise"—those who deeply repect God—will understand them. Those who are not truly pursuing a relationship with Jesus will be clueless as these things begin to unfold.

Prophecy Being Fulfilled. God told Daniel to seal up the prophecies **until the time of the end**. Indeed, they have been sealed, since most prophecies in past years were seen as outrageous by unbelievers. It was only the true followers of Jesus who believed these prophecies were real when they sounded impossibly ridiculous to everyone else. Certainly, they have been sealed until only recently.

We are finally beginning to understand many of the prophecies of Daniel today. So, what time, then, must we be in, if the prophecies are finally being unsealed? Remember what the prophecy said, "*seal up the book **until the time of the end**.*"

We do not yet completely understand all the prophecies of Daniel, but many of them we do. For example, several things mentioned in the last part of this very verse are obvious prophecy fulfillments today. We will look at them next.

> *Many of the prophecies we are beginning to understand. So, what time, then, must we be in?*

Everybody Ought to Know

Many Will Rush Here and There

Let's look at Daniel 12:4 again, *"But you, Daniel, keep this prophecy a secret; seal up the book until the time of the end,* **when many will rush here and there***, and knowledge will increase."*

God told Daniel to seal up the book until *the time of the end*. Then He proceeded to describe that time—*the time of the end*. He told Daniel that *many will rush here and there.* No one was rushing anywhere back in Daniel's day.

Prior to the industrial revolution that saw the invention of trains, planes, and automobiles, the average person never traveled more than thirty miles from the place where they were born. And they never traveled faster than a galloping horse could take them. But today...!

Need I make the case that people are *rushing here and there* today? That is a fair description of our daily lives, isn't it—always *rushing here and there?*

Prophecy Fulfilled. Though I have lived in Houston for over 25 years, I worked in Mexico City for several of those years. Every Monday morning I would board a plane that took me to another city in another country. Thursday evening I would board another plane to take me home. As I did so, I watched thousands of others doing the same as we all *rushed here and there.* I was only

> *Daniel 12:4*
> *...seal up the book until the time of the end, when many will rush here and there.*

one of thousands living in one country and working in another, while sleeping in our own beds four nights a week.

And what about freeway systems, bus and train stations and subways?

There is still more to this verse, though, and there is still more to the prophecy. The rest of this verse tells us that *knowledge will increase.*

Knowledge Will Increase

Once again, let's read the prophecy a final time. Daniel 12:4, *"But you, Daniel, keep this prophecy a secret; seal up the book until the time of the end, when many will rush here and there, and* **knowledge will increase.**"

To give some perspective, here, I should point out that it took 1,500 years for knowledge to double from the time of Christ. What they mean by "knowledge", is absolutely everything that mankind knows about everything.

Then, knowledge doubled again in just the next 500 years. As the industrial age began to develop, knowledge doubled again in just 250 years. I think you notice the trend here.

Prophecy Fulfilled. I remember reading an article in the 1990s that said that knowledge (science and technology) was doubling every 2 years. Then, only a few years later, I read another article that reported that knowledge was doubling in only 18 months. Most recently, I read an article at *industrytap.com* by David Russell Shilling, dated April 2013, with this headline, *Knowledge Doubling Every 12 Months, Soon to be Every 12 Hours.*

Not only is knowledge greatly increased, it is greatly increasing at a greatly increasing rate. It is to the point that it is beginning to scare people. If ChapGPT and AI doesn't have you a little bit worried, the threat of robots disrupting our lives maybe does. I think we can safely say that the prophecy has been fulfilled when it said, *knowledge will increase.*

Indeed, we see all the elements of this verse coming true all around us as we see human mobility greatly increased as well as a dramatic and growing expansion in science and technology. God is progressively revealing more and more of these prophecies about our present day—this period in history since the Jews returned to Israel. All, just as the prophecies predicted.

Wars, Famines & Earthquakes

Who is not aware of this prophecy in Matthew 24:7-8? It reads, *"Nation will go to war against nation, and kingdom against kingdom. There will be famines and earthquakes in many parts of the world. But all this is only the first of the birth pains, with more to come."*

The Bible is clear about the characteristics of these events. They are likened to birth pains which increase in both frequency and intensity.

Wars

Prophecy Fulfilled. Since we all know of the unprecedented wars of the last century, we won't spend time with those statistics except to remind ourselves that while World War I killed between 18 and 22 million people, World War II killed between 50 and 80 million people. Just that war, alone, killed a full three percent of the entire population of the planet. No previous war ever even came close.

In the scope of history, those wars were yesterday. We sadly seem on the verge of more to come. And the book that tells the future warns us there will be. The worst wars of all are still to come.

Famines

Famine, to most of us in the United States, is utterly unknown and

> *World War II alone, killed a full three percent of the entire population of the planet. No war before even came close.*

unless we have studied the subject, we are probably unaware of the horrific starvation suffered by tens of millions around the world in historically recent years. The numbers we will consider come from Wikipedia which lists famines going back to the time before Christ. The numbers of deaths, however, are understandably not available until you begin to approach the most recent centuries.

I'll give you the best estimated statistics for the last 300 years. These are very imprecise estimates due to the lack of data available. Nonetheless, we are still able to see the trend predicted in the prophecy—increased frequency and intensity.

Prophecy Fulfilled. During the 1700s Wikipedia lists 27 famines. Only nine of which, or 33%, record numbers of deaths. If we assume that the nine famines with statistics represent an average, we can very roughly estimate the total number of deaths at 105 million.

During the 1800s there were 33 recorded famines. Twenty-four of them, or 72% include records for the numbers of deaths. From that we can roughly extrapolate the total famine deaths for the 1800s to be about 120 million.

During the 1900s there were 58 recorded famines. Forty-five, or 78% of these famines include records for the numbers of deaths. Again, we can roughly estimate the total deaths from famine for the 1900s to be about 199 million. During the last century, famine has killed more people than all the record-breaking wars of that period.

Years	No. of Famines	Deaths
1700s	27	105 million
1800s	33	120 million
1900s	58	199 million

Luke 21:11 describes the prophecy this way, *"There will be great **earthquakes**, and there will be **famines** and **plagues** in many lands."*

Plagues

Modern times are not immune to plagues as we have seen with the coronavirus that has affected the entire planet. The Covid-19 pandemic has confronted the human race with the scary truth of just how vulnerable humanity really is.

Covid-19 was hardly the first such plague, as we are all aware of news over recent years concerning HIV, Ebola, Swine flu, Bird flu, SARS, and MERS. The United Nations warns that we should not think we have seen the last of such plagues. They tell us that we should expect more of this.

A recent UN report said, *"Experts expect to see a steady stream of these diseases jumping from animals to humans in the years ahead as habitats are ravaged by wildlife exploitation, unsustainable farming practices and climate change."* However, Covid-19 has shown us that the ugly truth about plagues is that our own species, mankind, is who we should probably be fearing the most.

Worldwide virus deaths are nothing new. The single event of the Spanish Flu of 1918 killed nearly 3% of the entire world's population.

Viruses are not the only plagues that we've seen recently, however. An article by Matt Simon published on February 5th, 2020 for Wired, was entitled, *The Terrifying Science Behind the Locust Plagues of Africa*. This and other articles describe it as "a plague of Biblical proportions" since "a swarm covering only 2 ½ football fields by 2 ½ football fields can eat as much food as 35,000 humans." As if that was not bad enough, here is the headline from an article in The Guardian, written by Samuel Okiror just two months later on April 20th, 2020 entitled, *Second Wave of Locusts in East Africa Said to be 20 Times Worse.*

Between 1900 and 1999, war, famine and disease killed over 10% of the world's total population. That was over 350 million people—greater than the entire population of the United States today and double the population of the US in 1950.

Earthquakes

Much more could be said about war, famine, and plagues, but now let's look at earthquakes. The statistics are truly startling. These earthquake statistics come directly from the US Geological Survey, US government website. You can find the following numbers for yourself at: https://earthquake.usgs.gov/earthquakes/search/

Prophecy Fulfilled. During the 50 years before Israel became a nation there were only 8,158 earthquakes worldwide that measured 2.5 or greater on the Richter Scale. During the 50 years after Israel became a nation there were 342,227 earthquakes that measured 2.5 or greater on the Richter Scale. And in just the first 20 years of this century, alone, there have already been 518,641 earthquakes that measured 2.5 or greater on the Richter Scale.

At the current rate, we can expect at least 1,296,602 earthquakes that measure 2.5 or greater on the Richter Scale between 2000 and 2049.

Let me reiterate those numbers since they are so dramatic. During the first 50 years of last century and the 50 years before Israel became a nation (1900 to 1949) there were roughly 8,000 earthquakes with a Richter Scale magnitude of 2.5 or greater. During the first 50 years of this century (2000 to 2049) we can expect AT LEAST 1,3000,000 earthquakes with a 2.5 or greater Richter Scale magnitude. (Extrapolated from the massive number (518,641) of earthquakes that have already occurred during just the first 20 years of this millennium.)

Let me juxtapose those numbers for you: 8 thousand vs. 1.3 million earthquakes during two separate fifty-year periods only 100 years apart.

While these are official United States Geological Survey statistics, we can probably assume some increase in the numbers due to improved seismic technologies. That, however, cannot nearly explain the enormous increase.

Earthquakes with a Richter magnitude > 2.5	
Period	No. of Earthquakes
1900-1949 (50 yrs)	8,158
1950-1999 (50 yrs)	342,227
2000-2019 (20 yrs)	518,641
2000-2049 (50 yrs)	1,296,602

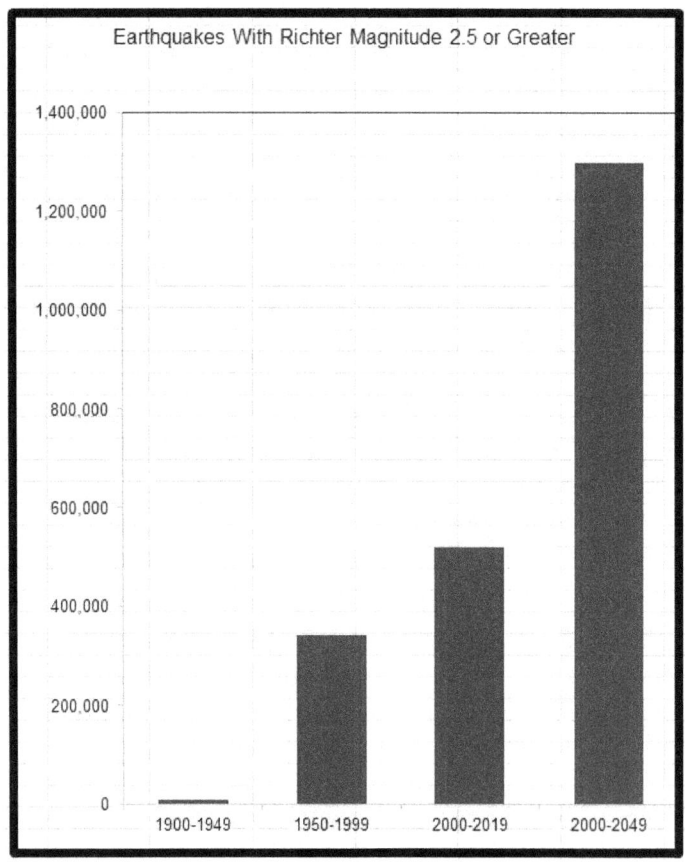

Interestingly, over the same period, large scale earthquakes, on the order of 7+ and 8+, have only doubled. This can only be seen as God's grace, mercy, and patience, because if these larger earthquakes had risen by the percentage of the smaller quakes, there would be few buildings standing anywhere on this planet. Still, such an increase in smaller earthquakes strikes an ominous tone of which we should all be aware.

> *Eight thousand compared to 1.3 million earthquakes during two separate fifty-year periods only 100 years apart.*

You see, seismic theory has recently shifted in a manner that bears noting. Up until very recently, the prevailing seismic wisdom held that small earthquakes released pressure, making the possibility of larger earthquakes less likely.

However, after the 6.4 earthquake in California on July 4th, 2019, followed by a 7.1 quake the very next day, a new understanding emerged. It is now believed that smaller earthquakes signal the possibility of larger ones. So, now the theory is that smaller earthquakes make larger earthquakes **more likely**, not less likely.

This is a Los Angeles Times headline from August 20th, 2019, *Scientists finally know how big earthquakes start: With many smaller ones.*

Well, the world has seen a tremendous increase in smaller earthquakes over the last fifty years. If this new seismic thinking is correct, to quote the Jerry Lee Lewis song, the world is in for "a whole lotta shakin' goin' on."

This should come as no surprise to anyone who studies the Bible, however. Revelation 6:12-14 says this, "*I watched as the Lamb broke the sixth seal,* **and there was a great earthquake***. The sun became as dark as black cloth, and the moon became as red as blood. Then the stars of the sky fell to the earth like green figs falling from a tree shaken by a strong wind. The sky was rolled up like a scroll,* **and all of the mountains and islands were moved from their places**."

While that verse is prophetic of a future earthquake, we are only concerned with currently fulfilling Bible prophecy in this book. Nevertheless, we do not want to be ignorant as to how current seismic events and science point to future prophecy fulfillments, as well.

On June 5th, 2020, I made a note of a Forbes story written by Suzanne Rowan Kelleher. She reported nearly 300 earthquakes in Yellowstone in the previous month of May.

> *"Scientists finally know how big earthquakes start: With many smaller ones."*

Although Yellowstone sits atop what is called a supervolcano, Suzanne explains that seismologists are more afraid of a large earthquake than an eruption. Oxford Dictionaries defines a supervolcano like this: "*an unusually large volcano having the potential to produce an eruption with major effects on the global climate and ecosystem.*"

For the fun of it, here are the statistics copied directly from Earthquaketrack.com, today, October 9, 2023.

0 earthquakes in the past 24 hours

5 earthquakes in the past 7 days

9 earthquakes in the past 30 days

262 earthquakes in the past 365 days

These are the sort of headlines that we all have become increasingly accustomed to reading in recent years.

Finally, we should not overlook the phrase, "*...earthquakes in many parts of the world...*" which we find in the prophecy from Matthew 24:7-8, which I'll restate here, "*Nation will go to war against nation, and kingdom against kingdom. There will be famines and* **earthquakes in many parts of the world**. *But all this is only the first of the birth pains, with more to come.*"

As you probably know, if you have been following seismic news over recent years, earthquakes are popping up everywhere, including places that have not seen seismic activity before—just like the prophecy foretold.

Everybody Ought to Know

Gospel Preached Worldwide

Here is what the prophecy says in Matthew 24:14, "And **this gospel of the kingdom will be proclaimed throughout the whole world** as a testimony to all nations, **and then the end will come.**"

There was a time when this prophecy seemed an impossibility—but not anymore. Certainly, though, we are not there, yet. Actually, I should say, "We are not *quite* there, yet."

I remember an experience I had during a trip to a remote area of Honduras. I was in search of people groups in remote areas with difficult access to the Gospel. I heard about the Tol Indian group deep in the mountains. I was on a motorcycle.

When I arrived there, I was confronted by a young Indian man about 30 years old. I am six feet tall. He was only about five feet tall, but he brandished a machete about the same size, which made him a bit taller than I. His demeanor was austere, bordering on hostile. He had many questions about who I was and what my intentions might be.

It turns out that there had been an attempt on the Indian chief's life. Someone had shot several bullets at his house from across the valley. This young man had been in the city at the time, far from these isolated mountains. He was one of just a handful of people from this tribe with his level of education. He spoke Spanish, in addition to his Indian dialect.

He considered it his responsibility to protect the chief, so he had returned from the city with his machete. Once he understood why I was there, I was warmly received, and we became friends.

Now comes the part relevant to this topic. While I was there in 1989, I learned that there was a Christian couple working to translate the New Testament into Tol, an unwritten Honduran Indian language. I did not get to meet them since they were away during the short period that I was in the village.

> There had been an attempt on the Indian chief's life. Someone had shot several bullets at his house from across the valley.

Let me share an interesting aside. We have some dear friends who knew and supported those missionary translators. They recounted to me one of the missionaries' many adventures while working with this Indian tribe.

During a trip out of this remote area, their vehicle broke down. The timing belt had broken. In case you are challenged in the area of automobile repair, let me tell you that a broken timing belt is a very, very bad thing. They had visiting friends with them and a baby, far from accommodations, paved roads, phones, running water, or electricity. Of course, there was no public transportation available, either. They spotted a poor house which represented the only shelter, so they went there.

As often was the case, they found people in great need. Someone in the house was gravely ill. The missionaries always carried medicines for such occasions. The wife returned to the vehicle to retrieve the medications. She reached her hand under the seat and felt something like a snake. It was not a snake. It was a timing belt!

Back to the prophecy of worldwide exposure to the Gospel...
There was a little schoolhouse in the village. The government was educating all the children in Spanish, the national language. Everyone under 30 years of age spoke Spanish, while many of the older folks were not yet fluent in it, at that time.

The New Testament translation into Tol was finished a short time later. The task remained, though, to teach the people to read this newly written language. In most cases the translators do not perform this task. It is left for other missionaries to do that.

Do you see the problem? Spanish was rapidly becoming the common language of the tribe. Only the older generation needed the new Bible translation, but they would have to be taught to read this newly written language first—a very, very tall order.

This experience occurred over 30 years ago. Here are the current statistics from Wikipedia. Today, the population of this Indian group is over 20,000, yet only 500 native speakers remained in 2012. By now, I would be surprised to find any tribal members who do not speak Spanish. If there are any, each day there will be less because of the influence of national language education—Spanish in this case—the intrusion of the outside world, and the passing of the elderly.

This is happening all over the world. Governments have been educating children in the national languages, and it has been steadily shrinking the world in terms of languages.

The Bible, however, already exists in all the national languages of the world. According to *www.ethnologue.com* a full 50% of the entire world population speaks one of only 23 national languages. They further explain that while there are 7,117 languages in the world (this estimate does not include sign languages), 40% of them are endangered because so few people speak them.

Many languages have less than 1,000 speakers and the number of languages falling into this group is growing daily as the number of people speaking remote languages is constantly shrinking as national languages become more dominant through education.

Nonetheless, there are a number of Christian organizations still dedicated to translating the Bible into the remaining languages of the world. Most of them are concerned with getting the written Scriptures into every language that has at least some minimum number of speakers.

> *50% of the entire world population speaks one of only 23 national languages.*

Here are some June 2020 statistics from the Wycliffe Global Alliance website: *wycliffe.net/wp-content/uploads/2019/11/2019_Bible_Translation_Statistics_EN.pdf* Over five and a half billion people in the world have the entire Bible in their language. Another 786 million people have the New Testament in their language, while an additional 470 million people have at least some portion of the Bible in their language. Today, language translation remains for only 171 million people, or less than 2.2% of the world's population.

Prophecy on the verge of fulfillment. While it once took years to translate the Bible into a new language, because of computers and new methods, the task can now be performed in several months. Needless to say, in terms of Bible translation into the languages of the world, light can be seen at the end of a very short tunnel.

Let's review the prophecy in Matthew 24:14, "And **this gospel of the kingdom will be proclaimed throughout the whole world** as a testimony to all nations, **and then the end will come**."

We have not even mentioned solar powered radios and audio players with the Bible in spoken word, which are being distributed by the tens of thousands in the most remote locations—and often in languages with no alphabet. Television and the Internet are also spreading the Gospel in a prolific way.

> *Bible translation remains for only 171 million people. Well over 7 billion already have all or some portion of the Bible.*

According to those dedicated to the translation of God's Word into the languages of the world, we are on the verge of that task being completed. Some say by 2035, others say even sooner.

You'll notice that the prophecy does not say that the Bible will be translated into all the languages of the world, but that the gospel would be *proclaimed throughout the whole world*. When that task is finally completed, what does the prophecy say will happen next?

Russia in the Middle East

Let us first read the prophecy in Ezekiel 38:1-9. *"This is another message that came to me from the LORD: 'Son of man, turn and face Gog of the land of Magog, the prince who rules over the nations of Meshech and Tubal, and prophesy against him. Give him this message from the Sovereign LORD: Gog, I am your enemy! I will turn you around and put hooks in your jaws to lead you out with your whole army. Persia, Ethiopia, and Libya will join you, too, with all their weapons. Gomer and all its armies will also join you, along with the armies of Beth-togarmah from the distant north, and many others.*

Get ready; be prepared! Keep all the armies around you mobilized and take command of them. **A long time from now** *you will be called into action.* **In the distant future you will swoop down on the land of Israel**, *which will be enjoying peace after recovering from war and after its people have returned from many lands to the mountains of Israel. You and all your allies—a vast and awesome army—will roll down on them like a storm and cover the land like a cloud."*

While this invasion of Israel has not yet happened, we can look at this prophecy for all the elements of it that have already occurred.

Job one is to identify the land of Magog. Josephus was a famous Roman historian from the time just after Christ. He wrote that Magog was the land of the nomadic Scythians who lived in the region north and northeast of the Black Sea and east of the Caspian Sea. That is exactly Russia today. Gog, as we can clearly see from Ezekiel 38, is the ruler of that land. Putin or his successor could very well be the ruler referred to as Gog.

Furthermore, Ezekiel 38:15 gives us the additional clue that the army of Gog, will come from Magog in the extreme north. *"You will come from your homeland in the distant north with your vast cavalry and your mighty army."* If you follow a line north from the tiny country of Israel, you will come directly to Moscow.

There are several things that we can already see in play from this still unfulfilled prophecy. One is Russia's interest in the Middle East.

Foreign Affairs magazine contained an article by Eugene Rumer, dated October 31, 2019, that began with this sentence, "Russia is on a roll in the Middle East." The article continued with this, "Russian airpower saved the Assad regime from certain defeat. Turkey and Israel must now accept the presence of Russian troops on their borders."

In fact, during the Syrian war that saw Russian intervention on the Assad regime's behalf, I stood on the Israeli-Syrian border on the Golan Heights, looking down on Syria, and heard the constant explosions of war in the distance.

> *"Turkey and Israel must now accept the presence of Russian troops on their borders."*

This Russian presence is a relatively new phenomenon as the article went on to explain. "The reemergence of Russia as a major power broker in the Middle East is striking not only in contrast with the United States' erratic posture in the region but because for a quarter century after the Cold War, Russia had been absent from the region." But not today!

Russia is extremely interested in the Middle East these days. But that's not all. As the prophecy indicates, Russia would form a military alliance with a host of nations of which Persia would be principal.

Iran was historically known as Persia until 1935. That is when Reza Shah, the Shah of Iran at the time, began to ask the world to refer to Persia as Iran, which has been its name ever since.

In those days Iran was a staunch friend and ally of the US. Before the Jimmy Carter presidency there was no chance that Iran would side with Russia and invade Israel. However, President Carter permitted the overthrow of the Shah of Iran and we all know the consequences to the world for that.

> *Before the Jimmy Carter presidency there was no chance that Iran would side with Russia and invade Israel.*

Iran has fought multiple proxy wars in the Middle East and Africa undermining the stability of the region. It has attacked its neighbors through proxy armies. It has fomented insurrection and political unrest in Iraq. It supports the terrorist organizations of Hamas, Hezbollah, and the Palestinian Islamic Jihad. Iran does not recognize Israel as a legitimate state and is committed to its obliteration. These are some of the consequences that the world is still dealing with today.

Russia and Iran now have a military alliance just like the prophecy foretold? Russia has, for years, been supplying Iran with nuclear technology in addition to a plethora of sophisticated weaponry which Iran has used to destabilize the Middle East.

What will happen when this Russian-led coalition of nations comes against Israel is beyond the scope of this book, but for the sake of the curious I'll give you the short version.

I'll let the Bible speak clearly for itself. Ezekiel 39:1-8 says, *"Son of man, prophesy against Gog. Give him this message from the Sovereign LORD: I am your enemy, O Gog, ruler of the nations of Meshech and Tubal. I will turn you around and drive you toward the mountains of Israel, bringing you from the distant north. I will knock the bow from your left hand and the arrows from your right hand, and I will leave you helpless.*

You and your army and your allies will all die on the mountains of Israel. I will feed you to the vultures and wild animals. You will fall in the open fields, for I have spoken, says the Sovereign LORD. And I will rain down fire on Magog and on all your allies who live safely abroad.

Then they will know that I am the LORD. *In this way, I will make known my holy name among my people of Israel. I will not let anyone bring shame on it.* **And the nations, too, will know that I am the LORD, the Holy One of Israel.** *That day of judgment will come, says the Sovereign LORD. Everything will happen just as I have declared it."*

Any questions?

God says He will do this for the same reason that He sent the ten plagues against Egypt and destroyed what was at that time the most formidable army in the world—and He did it to stun the world with the undeniable fact of His existence, His power, and His commitment to Israel.

People have forgotten *why* God smacked Egypt with ten plagues those many years ago, so He is about to remind everybody. But this time He will do it to an entire coalition of armies. He will leave no doubt in anyone's mind about His existence, His power, and His commitment to Israel. He's telling us ahead of time, *"And the nations, too, will know that I am the LORD, the Holy One of Israel."*

> *He did it to stun the world with the undeniable fact of His existence, His power, and His commitment to Israel.*

Russia and her allies invade Israel?

Dr. David Reagan, in his presentation, *50 Reasons Why We Are Living in the End Times*, praises the faith of believers of past years who accepted the Bible in spite of its seemingly impossible claims. Impossible claims then, maybe, but now they have become the very status quo!

> *People have forgotten why God smacked Egypt those many years ago, so He is about to remind everybody.*

Dr. Reagan explains that Dr. Cyrus Scofield, a Dallas pastor, published the first English study Bible in 1909. It was, and still is, widely used, today. Dr. Reagan points out that Dr. Scofield's first edition contained commentary about the verses from Ezekiel that we just read. Scofield wrote that the Bible states that in the end times Russia will invade Israel. He said he could not understand it because it made no sense at that time, but that he still had to believe it was true because the book that tells the future said so.

You see, in 1909 when Scofield published his study Bible, Russia was an orthodox Christian nation and the country of Israel hadn't existed for nearly 2,000 years. In 1909 it was preposterous to expect that an orthodox Christian nation would invade a country that did not even exist. Yet, how dramatically things have changed in the last 100 years to perfectly accommodate those prophecies.

Dr. Scofield died in 1921. How right he was to take the Bible seriously and literally for what it plainly said. Just 27 years after his death the United Nations drew Israel back on the map and Jews began to return there from all over the world—just as the prophecy predicted.

Furthermore, we see Russia in Syria today; and right on the border of Israel while it builds the very alliances mentioned in this prophecy from over 2,500 years ago.

Worldwide Simultaneous Observation

Here is another ancient prophecy that had to seem quite ridiculous until only recently. Multiple times the Bible states that the entire world would be able to simultaneously watch the same event.

Now that is not absurd to us today, but consider an unbeliever's reaction to such a prophecy any time prior to 1969. If you listen carefully, you can still hear the echo of all the mocking and scorn that was directed at followers of Jesus who accepted the prophecies by faith.

Revelation 1:7 says, "*Behold, He is coming with the clouds, and **every eye will see Him**...*" This verse, of course, is speaking of Christ's return to earth at the end of the Tribulation. It says that everyone will be able to see the event. This is not the only prophecy of this event. Jesus prophesied it Himself in Matthew 24, 30 when He said, "*At that time the sign of the Son of Man will appear in the sky, **and all the nations** of the earth will mourn. They **will see the Son of Man coming on the clouds of the sky, with power and great glory**.*"

> *If you listen carefully you can still hear the echo of all the mocking and scorn that was directed at followers of Jesus.*

Incidentally, what will the nations of the earth be mourning? Will they mourn that they had been so dismissive, even hostile, toward their own creator? Or will they, like Sodom and Gomorrah, mourn that the revelry is over and the consequences are beginning?

The return of Jesus is not the only event foretold to be seen the world over. Revelation 11:19 also says, *"And for three and a half days, **all peoples, tribes, languages, and nations will stare at their bodies**. No one will be allowed to bury them."*

This is a prophecy about something that has not happened yet. Since we are not concerned with future prophecy in this book, we'll not go into details of this event, except to note that the technology necessary for its fulfillment already exists. Again, we see a prophecy that the entire world will be able to simultaneously watch the same event.

Prophecy Fulfilled. The first worldwide television broadcast was the Apollo 11 moon landing in 1969. Of course, you would have needed to have access to a television set. Today, it is much easier. Anyone with a smartphone can livestream to the entire world via several platforms; the most popular being *YouTube* and *facebook*. In mere seconds, a child can do it. And anyone anywhere in the world with a smartphone can view in real time what is being presented, simply knowing the URL.

Commerce Controlled Centrally

This prophecy has not yet been fully fulfilled, but we can already see that technology exists for its fulfillment. Revelation 13:16-17 reads, *"Also it causes all, both small and great, both rich and poor, both free and slave, to be marked on the right hand or the forehead, so that **no one can buy or sell unless he has the mark**..."*

Up until very recently it would have been impossible to control sales and purchases the world over. But not today! According to this verse, such transactions will one day be controlled throughout the world.

Accommodating conditions for this prophecy. Welcome to the world of the Radio-Frequency Identification chip or RFID chip. It's your world today, after all. According to Wikipedia, in January of 1973, Mario Cardullo, an American inventor, patented the first primitive RFID device. Today it has been reduced to the size of a grain of rice and has been inserted into the hands of tens of thousands of people all around the world. It is currently being placed under the skin between the thumb and index finger.

With this chip, locks can be opened, medical and passport information can be stored, and business transactions can be made. Your keys, wallet, and personal information can all be contained in this tiny chip implanted under the skin of your hand. As technology advances, it can be expected that this chip will increase in functionality and be reduced in size even further—quite possibly something like an invisible tattoo that is being developed right now.

You should also know that there is a worldwide movement toward cashless economies. Sweden is well on its way to becoming completely cashless, with Finland, China, South Korea, the United Kingdom, and Australia not far behind.

Think of all the advantages of a cashless society. Illegal activities would be dealt a devastating blow. Furthermore, physical money costs a lot to store, transfer, produce, and protect. In fact, most coins are not worth the cost of the materials and manufacturing to create them. So many reasons to go to cashless economies!

> *Welcome to the world of the Radio-Frequency Identification chip or RFID chip. It's your world today, after all.*

I'm sure that everyone is aware that the United States experienced a national coin shortage post-Covid. In addition, the coronavirus has caused many businesses to stop accepting cash, adding one more motivation for a cashless society and a move to cryptocurrency. There is growing pressure, worldwide, to move to a single world cryptocurrency.

A cashless economy is a digital economy. If you marry an electronic economy with the RFID chip, think of the control that this would put into the hands of just a few. The technology of the RFID chip makes this prophecy fluidly possible. It is more than a possibility. It is even more than a probability. It is a certainty that you don't even need Bible prophecy to see is coming. Although it was the book that tells the future that predicted it thousands of years ago.

More and more companies are offering these chips to employees. Currently it is a voluntary option in most cases, but it is easy to see how this could soon become mandatory! At that point, all purchases could be controlled. If a person does not certify allegiance to a political leader, a government, an organization, or doctrine, their business transactions could be denied. Technology exists to do that right now.

Consider, for a moment, the absurdities of political correctness, Diversity, Equity and Inclusion (DEI), Corporate Social Responsibility (CSR), Critical Race Theory (CRT), Environmental, Social and Governance (ESG) and the "cancel culture" of today. How scary it would be if such onerous political and social values were *imposed* on every single individual. Again, the technology exists for this to happen today through control of commerce. It is soon coming to a world economy near you!

> *If a person does not certify allegiance to a political leader, a government, an organization, or doctrine, their business transactions could be denied.*

Now consider the dreadful control of the world that this technology will put into the hands of a coming world leader. Though outside the scope of this book, I will at least tell you his name—The Antichrist. Mind you, those not respectful of God will be oblivious as to his true identity and will see him as a savior.

Mount of Olives to Split in Half

The Bible, the book that tells the future, says that Jesus will physically return from Heaven to this planet from whence He departed 2,000 years ago. When He does, His feet will touch the Mount of Olives and the mountain will split in two. The Bible plainly explains that it will split from the east to the west with half the mountain moving north and half the mountain moving south.

This has not yet happened, of course, so why should it be included here? What evidence could there possibly be that this could actually happen? In order to answer that, let me share some information about the Mount of Olives.

The Mount of Olives is just east of the Temple Mount in Jerusalem. The Temple Mount sits atop Mount Moriah, where Abraham took Isaac in obedience to God's directive to sacrifice him. As crazy as that had to sound to Abraham at the time, he knew by faith what we all know now—God had a plan. God always has a plan for people who actively respect Him and His word—the Bible.

The Kidron Valley separates Mount Moriah/The Temple Mount from the Mount of Olives to the east. One can walk from the top of one to the top of the other in thirty minutes or so. I should mention that these are not mountains by Colorado standards. Someone who has seen the

> *Abraham knew by faith what we all know now—God had a plan.*

Rocky Mountains would call these "hills" by comparison.

Let's read the actual prophecy. Zechariah 14:4 says, "*And in that day His feet will stand on the Mount of Olives, which faces Jerusalem on the east. And* **the Mount of Olives shall be split in two**, *from east to west, making a very large valley; half of the mountain shall move toward the north and half of it toward the south.*"

Accommodating conditions for this prophecy. It turns out that there is a large fault that runs east to west across the summit of the Mount of Olives. In fact, the summit is somewhat distorted by the fault, making the peak not well defined because of a noticeable indentation.

The story of its discovery is that King Hussein of Jordan wanted to build the new Intercontinental Hotel atop the Mount of Olives in 1964. This was three years before the Six Day War of 1967, which saw the entire area pass to Israeli control. While preparing the site, the fault was discovered and so the hotel had to be moved further to the south. The hotel is currently called the Seven Arches Hotel.

The Mount of Olives and its fault sit ready for the Lord's return. All they need is the earthquake that the Bible tells us will accompany His second coming.

Increase in Sin, Immorality and Violence

The prophecies are numerous on the issue of the increased presence of evil and violence in society at the time of the Lord's return. We will look at just a few of them.

Matthew 24:12 speaks of the moral condition of society in the end times. The entire chapter of Matthew 24 explains what to expect at that time, but verse 12 says this, *"Sin will be rampant everywhere..."*

Prophecy Fulfilled. Anyone can see the increase in evil in the world compared to just fifteen years ago. Those who are over the age of fifty or sixty are stunned by the moral deterioration that they see.

Who would have thought, fifty years ago, that abortion would cost the lives of more than 65,000,000 American babies? (If you are concerned, you might appreciate this video: *www.youtube.com/watch?v=1o5iYWE5lME)*

Who would have thought, just ten years ago, that homosexuality and other deviancies would be so embraced by society that it would be acceptable for men to entertain young children, wearing provocative women's attire? Who would have thought, ten years ago, that a person would get to choose their gender and use whatever bathroom they chose?

Who would have thought, just ten years ago, that all the advancements that women had made in sports, would be summarily erased as biological men were allowed to compete against them, robbing them of their victories, awards and scholarships.

Who would have thought ten years ago, that advocates for pedophilia would be emboldened to go public? Who would have thought, just five years ago, that courts would begin to entertain leniency toward pedophilia and that the subject would begin to be dealt with flippantly in comedy? Welcome to this new America!

Meanwhile, prayer in school is bad, a child taking a Bible to school must be reprimanded, and the Ten Commandments or crosses must not be tolerated in public.

If you hesitate to believe that it has come to this, then consider Bremerton, Washington's football coach, Joseph Kennedy, who was put on leave when he simply knelt to pray on the field after the game. It took debate in the Supreme Court of the United States of America to restore Mr. Kennedy's job.

> *But prayer in school is bad, a child taking a Bible to school must be reprimanded, and the Ten Commandments or crosses mustn't be allowed in public.*

Can you imagine this in a country where our founding father, John Adams said this, *"Our Constitution was made only for a moral and religious people. It is wholly inadequate to the government of any other."*

Who gets to say what's right and wrong?

Societies cannot be the final arbiters of what is and what is not sin. Otherwise, depending on where you live in the world, brutal slavery could be just fine, public beheadings customary, and barbarity against women, acceptable conduct. That's what fickle social mores give you.

Fortunately, God's injunctions are not capricious. His directives do not change. His word is firm and dependable in every era of time. Consider Psalm 111:7 that reminds us, *"...all His laws are trustworthy."* And verse 10 which says, *"A respect for God is where wisdom starts; all who follow His instructions have a proper understanding of things."*

In contrast to God's consistency and steadfastness, societies follow the whims of constantly morphing cultures that presumptuously pass laws that legalize sin as they pass others that criminalize righteous behavior.

How "fortuitous" for those who successfully pressure society to legalize their sin. The pedophile has watched as society succumbed to pressure from abortionists and homosexuals. He has been patiently awaiting his turn.

> *The pedophile has watched as society succumbed to pressure from abortionists and homosexuals. He has been patiently awaiting his turn.*

And his patience is paying off. In 2020, Netflix produced the movie *Cuties*, directed by the French-Senegalese director, Maïmouna Doucouré. She won the Directing Award at the Sundance Film Festival on January 23rd 2020. The movie depicts a dance troupe of 11-year-old girls doing the most sexualized moves you can imagine. And as if the dancing moves were not disturbing enough, the camera angles were most indecent.

Finally, just what pedophiles have been hoping for—their perversion finding an acceptable place in society too.

While the movie received some push-back from voices that still have a moral compass, it has received wide acclaim and strong defense by Hollywood and all the usual suspects in media and politics that rationalize such things as "empowering to women."

And if you're thinking the opposition to it is probably an overreaction by stuffy Christians, I wager you wouldn't think so if you have an adolescent daughter of your own and ever had the misfortune to see it yourself. The desensitized conscious, though, may still not recognize the perversion of it all. I watched a report on a TV news program and saw more of the movie than I would wish to see. The report claimed to not be showing the most graphic scenes.

To think that it is an alarmist notion to believe that pedophilia could one day be tolerated—even protected—think again. It was not that long ago that such a movie would have brought criminal charges. It was not that long ago that the ideas of abortion and same-sex marriage were anathema.

When the Jewish nation of Judah was at the point where God called their sin "*an incurable wound*" (Jeremiah 30:12), He promised judgement on them that no repentance could stop. In Isaiah 5:20 He condemned the social standards that existed by saying, "*Woe to those who call evil good and good evil, who put darkness for light and light for darkness, who put bitter for sweet and sweet for bitter!*"

Is that not what we see happening in the most glaring terms in the United States today? What else do you call arresting pastors for opening the doors of their churches during the Corona virus, but allowing bars to be open or thousands to roam the streets in tight proximity while destroying cars, burning down buildings and killing people? Is that not the very definition of "calling evil, good and good, evil?"

If Judah, God's chosen people, had exceeded God's patience, then where must the US be on the scale of God's tolerance for sin—especially after this country, like Israel of old, has been so blessed by Him? When a society loses its last vestiges of morality, God must step in at some point.

> *If God's chosen people had gone beyond the end of God's patience, then where must the US be on the scale of God's tolerance for sin?*

Here is a verse tucked away in Psalm 11:3 that is most applicable today. It says, "*If the foundations are destroyed, what can the righteous do?*"

Do you understand the significance of what that verse is warning us about? Is it not true that when a society no longer knows the difference between good and evil or right and wrong, it becomes impossible for a righteous person to make a case? How can you make a case for what is right and good and fair when society has come to believe that it is wrong and bad and unfair? Are we not already there, with upside down values becoming mainstream all around us?

Again, Matthew 24 says this in verse 37, *"For as were the days of Noah, so will be the coming of the Son of Man."* Well, what was it like in the days of Noah? Genesis 6:11-12 tells us, *"Now God saw that the earth had become **corrupt and was filled with violence**. God observed all this corruption in the world, for everyone on earth was corrupt."*

Everyone was corrupt. Everyone did just as they pleased. Violence was rampant. How is America any different today, with frequent mob lootings, politicians being assaulted on our streets and laws being changed to reduce or remove criminal penalties for it all?

I'll spare you a lot of statistics since I'm sure that we are all aware of the huge increase in crime and homicides in America since the demonstrations and violence that began after the George Floyd incident. Even before that, though, general security in American society had been deteriorating for decades.

Years ago, people left their homes and cars unlocked. Years ago, parents would let their children roam the neighborhoods. Years ago, people did not feel the urgent need for personal protection. Years ago, people picked up hitchhikers and stopped to help people broken down on the road. Years ago, people did not distrust everyone.

Evil gets organized

At one end of the political spectrum is Fascism which must account for the murder of millions of Christians and Jews. And history tells us that Hitler and those around him were involved in the occult as well.

At the other end of the political spectrum is Marxism, which is another satanic ideology that accounts for more murdered Christians in the last 100 years than any other philosophy or religion, including Fascism and radical Muslims. We are speaking of tens of millions of murdered Christians. A hatred for the God of the Bible is at the root of Marxism.

Influential political activists like Patrisse Cullors and Alicia Garza proudly claim to be "trained Marxists." They are co-founders of Black Lives Matter. Just one of the places that Ms. Cullors confirms her Marxist roots in her own words, is here:
https://www.youtube.com/watch?v=HgEUbSzOTZ8

Even more alarming still, is what she candidly explained in a 2015 interview with Melina Abdullah, professor of African Studies at California State University, Los Angeles. Ms. Cullors explained that she routinely communicates with the dead and that the dead inform, in no small way, all her activities. A description of the ancestor worship roots of BLM can be found in this Georgetown University

Berkley Center article: https://berkleycenter.georgetown.edu/responses/the-fight-for-black-lives-is-a-spiritual-movement

Ephesians 6:12 is informative about who the real enemy is, as we noted in a previous chapter. Again, it says, *"For we do not wrestle against flesh and blood, but against the rulers, against the authorities,* **against the cosmic powers** *over this present darkness,* **against the spiritual forces of evil in the supernatural realm**.*"*

When Patrisse Cullors thinks she is communicating with the dead, just who do you think she is really communicating with? You can be sure it is *"the spiritual forces of evil in the supernatural realm,"* as the verse warns, posing as the passed relatives to whom she thinks she is speaking. Like Fascism, wherever Marxism exists, it brings a virulent hatred of God and a cozy acceptance of the occult.

> *Wherever Marxism exists it brings a virulent hatred of God and a cozy acceptance of the occult.*

Consider the destruction, violence, and death that has been the result of BLM activities. How cleverly evil the devil is. Here we have a noble name and a noble cause co-opted by transmundane occultism with Marxist roots and goals.

Large corporations are putting millions and millions of dollars into the hands of such people. Are they so unknowing of what they are promoting and where this will all end? Even worse, maybe they are not unknowing at all!

One more thing

In closing this topic, I will reiterate how God hates violence. He has dealt definitively with every violent society in history. Naturally, God considers killing babies to be extreme violence, too. In Judah, even the king sacrificed his son to the pagan god, Molech, for good luck. 2 Kings 21:6 says, *"**Manasseh also sacrificed his own son in the fire**. He practiced sorcery and divination, and he consulted with mediums and psychics. He did much that was evil in the LORD's sight, arousing his anger."*

Today our society violently sacrifices its children for the sake of convenience and calls it "women's rights." God hates the taking of innocent life.

Godliness, fidelity, morality, and righteousness are now characteristics of a bygone era. They are no longer embraced or seen as truly respected virtues by most of society today. It is just as the Bible prophecies said it would be.

Increase in Materialism

2 Timothy 3:2, *"For people will love only themselves and their **money**. They will be boastful and proud, scoffing at God, disobedient to their parents, and **ungrateful**. They will consider nothing sacred."*

This prophecy mentions much more than just materialism. It mentions things that we all see at epidemic levels all around us today. Let's take a moment, though, to consider the sin of materialism listed here.

Money can buy "stuff." People love "stuff" so people love money.

Prophecy Fulfilled. What do people live for today? How many would say they live to glorify God? How many would say that they feel driven to share the Gospel of Jesus Christ with as many others as possible, because He deserves that people love Him back for what He did for them at the cross? How many people would say that they want desperately to raise their children to respect God and have a personal relationship with Him at the earliest age possible? How many people would say that they are profoundly saddened that after all Jesus endured at the cross, this world would be so blasphemously dismissive of Him? How many would say it grieves them when they consider His feelings—the hurtfulness of the rejection He so unfairly suffers?

> *Money buys "stuff". People love "stuff" so people love money.*

How many people would say that the sinful culture around them steals their joy and is distressful to them? How many would say that they genuinely long for the day Jesus returns?

Yes, some would, but not many. In fact, way too few even in our churches today.

Sadly, what most people live for today is "stuff." They are consumed with getting it, getting more of it, protecting it, and showing it off. Oh, they flatter themselves that they are good citizens because they pay their taxes, pay their bills, and raise their children.

While there are genuine followers of Jesus who continually and sacrificially give to others what they have worked hard for, the materialistic person will only occasionally part with the tiniest fraction of what they have—a pittance that they will never miss—and they think they are Mother Teresa.

Little of what they are concerned with or motivated by, could seriously be considered "eternal values"—and certainly not eternal values as God defines them.

> *How they flatter themselves. When they occasionally give the tiniest pittance away and think they are Mother Teresa.*

No! They live for "stuff." Getting "stuff" is what fulfills them. Getting "stuff" even motivates their seemingly responsible behavior as they work hard so that they can get even more "stuff." This obsession with "stuff" is the very definition of materialism.

Increase in Materialism

The list of evils in 2 Timothy 3:2, also includes ingratitude. "*They will be boastful and proud, scoffing at God, disobedient to their parents, and **ungrateful**.*" Ingratitude is loathsome and repugnant. The English language denies me sufficiently negative superlatives to describe the heinous obscenity that is ingratitude. It not only demonstrates covetousness but the worst kind of selfishness, entitlement, and thanklessness as well.

Ingratitude is a reaction to a gift, not to something earned. Americans have so much compared to the rest of the world and compared to the rest of history. And in many cases, much of what people have was not earned, but acquired through inheritance, government programs or the generosity of others. Ingratitude is a truly despicable characteristic that thrives in society today.

I remember one day in 2003, stopping to speak with an able-bodied man, about thirty years of age, holding a sign that said, "Will work for food." I told him I was working in the yard and needed a little help. He asked how much I would pay him. I told him $10/hr., well above minimum wage at the time. He told me that he could get that much by begging and turned me down.

I remember the morning after Hurricane Rita hit Houston in 2005. It was one of the ten most intense hurricanes ever recorded. Thousands of people were stranded on highways leaving town after their gas ran out in the massive traffic jams that occurred. Gas stations were empty or had no power for their pumps.

I had several five-gallon cans of gas in my garage. I took them and some sandwiches out to I-45 north of Houston the next morning. By then, good Samaritans had helped many cars move on. I found one man still sitting beside the road. He said he lived about 20 miles further south and was out of gas. I gave him a sandwich and five gallons of gas so that he could return home. I left to help others. I watched as he allowed one Good Samaritan after another add to his trove of food and gasoline.

On the occasion of another disaster, my wife was manning a food bank, giving out generous bags to the needy. So that more people could be served, the recipients were instructed that each person was entitled to one bag only. Shockingly, there were more than a few who openly defied the rules and selfishly attempted to go from one line to another in order to receive additional bags, callous to the fact that others would then receive nothing. Such selfishness is repugnantly reprehensible.

Does idolatry exist today?

Let me share one other curious note on this topic of materialism. Having read the Bible through many, many times, I used to be puzzled by references to idolatry in the last days. After all, people don't bow down to metal and wood figurines anymore, do they? Certainly not in first world countries! Then I read this verse: Colossians 3:5, *"Put to death, therefore, whatever belongs to your earthly nature: sexual immorality, impurity, lust, evil desires and* **greed, which is**

idolatry." Galatians 5:5 says the same with these words, *"For of this you can be sure: No immoral, impure or **greedy person** — **such a man is an idolater** — has any inheritance in the kingdom of Christ and of God."*

Then it began to make sense. The *idolatry* of the last days is *greed*. Since *greed* is *idolatry*, who would deny that we live in an *idolatrous* culture, since we live in such a greedy and materialistic one? We live in a culture with an obsession for "stuff." People worship what they live for. If people are living for "stuff," then that's what they are worshipping. That's *idolatry*.

If you are not living for God, then you are just living for "stuff." It can be power, fame, control, knowledge, possessions, or anything else that is not of eternal consequence. If it is not of eternal value (and I mean eternal value according to God's standards, not ours), then it is just "stuff."

> *People live for what they worship. If people live for "stuff" then that's what they worship.*

There is nothing wrong with "stuff." There is just something wrong with *living* for "stuff" when we should be living for God. Though it may be unclear what it means to "live for God," I expect that one second after death it won't be unclear at all. It will just be too late to do anything about it.

The antidote to living for "stuff"

A person who is living for "stuff" is just killing time till they die since they are not doing anything of eternal significance. They are not investing in anything that will serve them well in eternity. What regret and remorse they will one day feel!

> *A person who is living for "stuff" is just killing time till they die.*

Need I remind you that a miraculous and spectacular book that tells the future says so?

The wise person invests in their future. The *really* wise person invests in their *eternal* future, too.

Are you looking for meaning in life beyond acquiring and managing your "stuff"? Genesis 1:27 says something about your purpose for existing. It reads, "*So God created man in his own image, in the image of God he created him.*"

God created man in His own image to the extent that man and God can communicate, and they both share the same emotions, the Bible tells us. God created man to have a relationship with him.

What greater meaning could exist in this universe than being able to call its creator, your friend? And He is not a friend without benefits, either. In Matthew 6 He says, "*Make your relationship with Me your number one priority, and I'll take care of everything else in your life that used to stress you out.*"

Increase in Christian Martyrdom

There have been Christian martyrs throughout history. Even before believers were called Christians, there were godly martyrs.

We can read about the very first one as early as the 4th chapter of the Bible. Genesis 4 describes how Abel brought an offering that was humbly respectful of God's will. Abel's older brother, Cain, brought an offering reflective of his pride and personal achievement. God was pleased with Abel's offering, but not so much with Cain's. So, Cain killed Abel, and the killing of people who want to follow God has never stopped.

Matthew 24:9 warns, *"Then they will deliver you up to tribulation and put you to death, and you will be hated by all nations for My name's sake."*

John 16:2 foretells, *"Indeed, the hour is coming when whoever kills you will think he is offering service to God."* (The thousands of Christians that ISIS has recently killed were all murdered in the name of the Muslim god.)

Revelation 6:9-11 describes the martyrdom that will finally trigger Christ's return, *"When he opened the fifth seal, I saw under the altar the souls of those who had been slain for the word of God and for the witness they had borne. They cried out with a loud voice, 'O Sovereign Lord, holy and true, how long*

> So, Cain killed Abel, and the killing of people who want to follow God has never stopped.

before you will judge and avenge our blood on those who dwell on the earth?'

Then they were each given a white robe and told to rest a little longer, until the number of their fellow servants and their brothers should be complete, who were to be killed as they themselves had been."

Prophecy Fulfilled (and it's not over yet). Let me share some numbers with you. Under "Christian Martyrs", *wikipedia.com* lists hundreds of Christians by name, who have been killed for their faith over the last 2,000 years. Among those names, though, there are listings like these that represent sometimes dozens, sometimes, hundreds, sometimes thousands, and sometimes even millions of Christian martyrs:

    Sri Lankan martyrs, 2019

    Sutherland Springs martyrs, 2017

    Alexandrian martyrs, 2017

    Cairo martyrs, 2016

    Algerian Martyrs, 1994-1996

    Ugandan Martyrs, 1885-1887

    Korean Martyrs, 1839, 1846, 1866

    etc.

But that's not all. Under the *wikipedia.com* heading of "Persecution of Christians in the Soviet Union," we find additional shocking statistics of brutality against Christians. Between 1917 and 1991, the Communist Party of Russia (and then the Soviet Union) destroyed churches and harassed, incarcerated, and executed religious leaders. According to the article, 106,300 Russian clergymen were executed during just the Great Purge of 1936-38.

That, however, does not begin to tell the story of Christian martyrdom during the last century. Quoting from the article we read, "Some sources estimate the total number of Christian victims under the Soviet regime to be between 12 and 20 million."

> *106,300 Russian clergymen were executed just during the Great Purge of 1936 to 1938.*

We have not even mentioned China or North Korea whose harsh persecution of Christians continues to this day and whose martyrs number in the millions. And what about the unspeakable cruelty of ISIS and Boko Haram in very recent years?

History is full of atrocities against the followers of Jesus. For example, in the thirty years leading up to 1570, countless Protestant Christians were murdered in Europe because they wanted to break away from the Catholic Church. Countless more perished during the many Roman Catholic Inquisitions. These include the Episcopal Inquisition, the Papal Inquisition, the Goa Inquisition, the Peruvian Inquisition, the Mexican Inquisition, and the mother of all inquisitions, the Spanish Inquisition.

The Church of England was likewise bathed in the blood of believers who just wanted to worship God or read the Bible in their own language.

Yes, people who have wanted to follow Jesus have found devil-inspired persecution throughout history. Much of it came from religious types who were certainly not people with a humble personal relationship with Jesus. Once again, we see the stark contrast between religion and relationship. One kills and the other accepts martyrdom. What could be more opposite?

Population Explosion

While the Bible does not specifically use the words, "population explosion," it does describe the same in Revelation 9:16 when it reports the size of a future army. "*I heard the size of their army, which was 200 million mounted troops.*"

While China does not have a 200-million-man army today, it could easily field one if it chose to, with its population of 1.5 billion.

India, too, has a population approaching 1.5 billion. These are the two most populous countries in the world.

You might find it interesting to know that the United States is the 3rd most populous country in the world, but has a population less than ¼ of either of the leading two countries.

It should not be overlooked, however, that the Muslims could also field an army of 200 million if all the Muslim nations pooled their populations of military service age.

The population estimates of the world at the time of Christ range from 200 to 400 million. All statistical sources agree that the population explosion that we now see in the world did not start until the early 1800's. Before that, due to infant mortality, uncontrolled disease and harsh living conditions, the population estimates of the world remained below 1 billion.

So, at the time this prophecy was made, which speaks of an army of 200 million, there was only about that number of human beings on the entire planet. What a bizarre prediction that must have seemed ridiculous until only recently. After all, an army as big as the entire population of the world at that time? How preposterous!

This prophecy distinctly suggests a population explosion the likes of which the world had never seen nor would see for 1,800 years. And it should not escape your notice that this 200-million-man army does not come from the south or the west or the north of Israel, but from the east where the only countries that could field such an army exist. (Revelation 16:12 refers to them as the "Kings of the East.")

At the time of this prophecy, that speaks of an army of 200 million, there was only about that many human beings on the entire planet.

Once again, for 2,000 years this prophecy must have been a source of derision and ridicule from all unbelievers. But today we can see its fulfillment as a distinct possibility.

So What?

Beyond settling the questions concerning the integrity and authenticity of Scripture, an appreciation for prophecy has other inestimable value, as well.

When you consider all the prophecies currently being fulfilled, some of which we have enumerated, you can come to no other conclusion than this: *If all that the Bible has said would happen up to this time, has indeed happened, why would I not believe the rest of such a book?*

How boneheaded would it be to see that all the Bible has predicted up to this point has come true, but then not believe its message or what it has to say about what comes next? How could I ignore what a book that tells the future says about God, about hell, about heaven and how to get there, when it has proven itself repeatedly through currently fulfilling Bible prophecy that I can verify with my own eyes?

How could I not accept the message of such a unique and miraculous book that tells the future, especially when that message is a most incredible love story? It is a story of an indescribable love that would compel our Creator to accept an undeserved martyrdom in order to extend to us the possibility of avoiding the eternal consequences of our sin. Who would ever believe such a love story if it did not come from a book that tells the future?

Time is running out

The Bible also places nearly all the prophecies being fulfilled today in the context of Christ's return to earth. While currently fulfilling prophecy builds our faith and confidence in the Bible, it should also remind us that Jesus' return is fast approaching. We do not know WHEN it will happen, but we can be certain THAT it will happen; and that the event is fast approaching. The Bible is clear that these currently fulfilling prophecies signal the proximity of Christ's return.

Knowing this with the certainty that we do, are we not motivated to be better prepared for His return? Are we not anxious to minimize regrets that we would otherwise have at that time?

I remember reading about an Indonesian Christian man who was seriously wounded, and whose wife was killed, when Muslims attacked his church. I was particularly struck by his statement that he was glad to have survived so he could better prepare himself to meet the Lord. That's not a ridiculous notion considering the Lord's own warning to us in Revelation 22:12 which says, *"Behold, I am coming soon, bringing my rewards with me, to repay each one of you for what he has done."*

To be clear, this was written to, and applies only to true believers. Believers will be rewarded for their faithfulness since they are forgiven of their sins. Unbelievers must sadly pay the eternal consequences for their sin, since they never repented, developed a relationship with Jesus, nor were forgiven. So says the book that tells the future.

Can you believe this?

A Life Way Research Survey in 2017 reported that 66% of children from Christian homes quit going to church between the ages of 18 and 22. While it is true that a small percentage of them return in later years, the question remains as to why they left in the first place.

The reasons cited in the survey included:
- *Moving away to college*
- *Church members were judgmental or hypocritical*
- *Felt no connection to others in church*
- *Disagreement on political/social issues*
- *Work responsibilities*

Do you see anything wrong with that list? Such motives for abandoning church seem woefully shallow, even petty. They are blind to the true cause. The cited reasons are not reasons at all, but simply *symptoms* of the actual problem.

> *66% of children from Christian homes quit going to church between the ages of 18 and 22.*

In fact, it is befuddling that a presumably Christian organization would be so unaware of the spiritual implications of their survey questions and therefore explain its findings in purely temporal terms, apparently oblivious to the real issue—the heart.

Tell me honestly, what percentage of children from Christian homes do you think would abandon church if they had a deep, personal, and dependent relationship with the

Lord Jesus Christ? After all, the objective is not just "going to church," completing confirmation classes or performing some other religious ritual. God's objective, clearly and repeatedly described in the Bible, is that we develop a real and personal relationship with Him.

I once asked Eunice, a high school senior, if there was any chance that she would become such a statistic when she left for college. She had a genuine relationship with the Lord like I've described. Eunice looked at me incredulously, as if hurt by the question, and said, "He is my Rock."

The next year she left for a university in Japan on an impressive scholarship. Though finding fellow believers is a bit more challenging in Japan, her faith only grew through her university experience. But, again, she had a deep, personal, and dependent relationship with the Lord to start with.

Now contrast that with Jonathan Steingard. He was the lead singer for a Christian music band, who in May of 2020, told the world that despite growing up in church, being the son of a pastor, and the lead singer of a Christian band, he had come to realize that he did not believe in God, after all.

There exists this absurd assumption that if you believe in God, that makes you a Christian. How preposterous! Look what James 2:19 says: *"You believe that God is one. You do well; the demons also believe, and shudder."* Does believing make the demons Christians, too? Of course not! What the demons do not have that real believers have, is a repentant heart and a deep, personal, dependent, and submissive relationship with God—something Jonathan Steingard apparently never had, either.

If the extent of Jonathan's Christianity was that he once believed in the existence of God, then he was no more a true Christian and follower of Jesus than the devil is. May I paraphrase James 2:19 a bit, which says, *"So, you think it's enough to believe God exists? Good for you. So do the demons, except that they tremble at the thought."*

> *There exists this absurd assumption that if you believe in God, that makes you a Christian.*

I'm sure that there are many people praying for Jonathan Steingard. His story may not be over yet. That's the beautiful thing about Jesus. While you have breath, you have hope. When your breath stops, so does your hope. Some other beautiful things about Jesus are that He is merciful, forgiving, patient, and gives second, third, and fourth chances.

If Jonathan had known that currently fulfilling Bible prophecy thoroughly establishes the integrity of the Bible, would he still have said what he did? Or, maybe one day he just decided that he preferred his sin and independence from God, more. Either way, it seems that he never really knew Jesus.

This is a classic example of the difference between religion and a genuine and personal relationship with Jesus Christ. Again, religion and relationship are vastly different things. To conflate the two—to not understand the difference—is to be terribly naïve and to be hornswoggled by the devil's deception.

Some just don't get it. Some just don't want to.

I am baffled how a person can grow up in church and not get it—not understand what it means to have a deep, personal, and dependent relationship with Jesus. Then again, maybe I shouldn't be so surprised, since I know there are many churches that don't explain what that means very well, or maybe don't explain it at all.

Sorrowfully, there are many church people who do not have a genuine relationship with Jesus. In fact, maybe they don't even know what it means to have one. As a result, they might one day find themselves doing what Jonathan Steingard did.

This can especially happen to people from religious systems that stress allegiance to the religious system instead of allegiance to Jesus. Chances are these religious systems probably don't teach all the indisputable evidences for the existence of God and the validity of the Bible, either.

A reason to believe

Before a person can develop a deep, personal, and dependent relationship with Jesus, they need to be convinced that the Bible is true. They need to know that they can trust what it says. They must somehow get past the cognitive dissonance caused by the conflicting and foolish spiritual theories that exist on all sides, as well as the social antagonism against the God of the Bible. They need to know that they can, without reservation, believe its message.

What better proof for the trustworthiness of the Bible is there than the current fulfillment of a myriad of ancient Bible prophecies occurring right now? Certainly, there are many other conclusive evidences for the genuineness of the Bible, as well; from scientific to historical to archeological to geographical to literary and even astronomical proofs. However, many of those authentications require some education to be able to understand, and are maybe not as simple, or as easily understood, or as convincing as currently fulfilling Bible prophecy.

Think About This

In 1803, Robert Fulton approached Napoleon about his new invention. The steamship could give Napoleon the means to defeat the British. Napoleon's reaction was, "You would make a ship sail against the wind and currents by lighting a bonfire under her decks? I pray you excuse me. I have no time to listen to such nonsense." It was beyond his ability to imagine or grasp the concept. He subsequently lost the war.

When you talk about spiritual things today, there are many who are uncomfortable with the subject, and dismiss it for the same reason that Napoleon rejected Fulton's help—it appears beyond their ability to grasp it.

In 1939, Leo Szilard, a brilliant Jewish physicist immigrant from Germany, was afraid that the Germans would develop an atomic bomb and dominate the world. He persuaded Albert Einstein to co-sign a letter urging President Roosevelt to finance research to develop the bomb first. Leo got Alexander Sachs, an economist and friend of his, to approach FDR with the letter, since Sachs was a friend of the president.

Like Napoleon blew off Robert Fulton and his steamship idea, Roosevelt blew off the idea of developing a nuclear bomb. It was beyond his ability to grasp the concept. As Sachs turned for the door, Roosevelt felt he might have offended his friend, so he invited him back for coffee the next day.

The next day Sachs reminded FDR of Napoleon's mistake that resulted in his defeat 100 years earlier. With the example that, "just because you don't understand something doesn't mean it's not true," FDR accepted the idea by faith, and the Manhattan project, the bomb, and the end of World War II were the results.

FDR needed the example of Napoleon to realize that things that may seem unlikely can be very real. Currently fulfilling Bible prophecy gives the open-minded unbeliever the proof they need to realize that what may seem unlikely to them (the truth of the Bible), is in fact, very real.

All religions lead to the same place?

Incidentally, the idea that all religions take you to the same place is actually correct—but with one exception. Since all religions, with the exception of one, have the same basic belief that Heaven/Nirvana/Swarga is achieved by being a good person and following the rules of the religion, they all share the same destination. Since they all point you down the same path, they will obviously all take you to the same place. With the exception of the one that is really a relationship instead of a religion, they all insist that compliance with their religious rituals coupled with good works, will get you into their "heaven."

In contrast, the message of the Bible stands apart with verses like Ephesians 2:8-9 that say, *"For by grace you have been saved through faith. And this is **not your own doing**; it is the gift of God, **not a result of works**, so that no one may boast."* And Isaiah 64:6 which says, *"We are all infected* *and impure with sin. When we display our righteous deeds, they are nothing but filthy rags. Like autumn leaves, we wither and fall, and our sins sweep us away like the wind."*

These verses confront the belief of all other religions—that mankind is basically good and can achieve heaven by being nice.

Only one path says that good works will **not** get you into heaven. While all the rest promote good deeds as the way to get into heaven, the path described in the book that tells the future says that only the blood of Jesus can satisfy the eternal consequences of sin for the humble person who turns to follow Jesus and develops a relationship with him.

> *These verses confront the belief of all other religions—that mankind is basically good and can achieve heaven by being nice.*

Easy, but not so simple.

I remember a conversation with a Muslim imam. He explained to me what it takes to become a Muslim. There are five rituals, or Pillars as they call them.

1) The Shahada (declaration of faith). "There is no god but Allah, and Muhammad is the messenger of Allah."
2) Salah (daily prayers). Five times daily and contain certain rituals.
3) Zakat (almsgiving). Again, certain rules surround this ceremonial practice.

4) Sawm (fasting). During the daylight hours of the month of Ramadan.
5) Hajj (pilgrimage). At least one visit to Mecca during the 12th month of the lunar calendar.

That makes you a Muslim. Other religions have other rites and rituals that earn you membership with them.

It is really not so simple for followers of Jesus. Sure, believers have disciplines, but they are voluntary actions that are the result of a changed heart, not required demands of a religious structure. I Samuel 16:7b says, *"...man looks on the outward appearance, but God looks on the heart."*

In John 4:24, Jesus, Himself, gave instruction as to how a person must approach God. He said, *"God is spirit, and those who worship him must worship in spirit and truth."*

Once again, we see the contrast between the outward rituals of religions vs. the personal intimacy of a relationship with Jesus.

Believers vs. Unbelievers

It is important that these terms be properly defined and understood. When speaking of "believers" and "unbelievers" as Biblical terms, we need to get our definitions from the Bible and not from society or our personal assumptions. When the book that tells the future speaks of a "believer", what exactly does it mean? The Bible is clear about the characteristics of a true believer.

A true believer...
a. Loves God above all else, with a desire to read the Bible in order to know Him better.
b. Deeply appreciates Jesus' sacrifice.
c. Feels compelled to obey Him.
d. Has the desire to learn more about Him.
e. Develops an enhanced sensitivity to and discomfort for sin.
f. Develops a genuine love for others.
g. Is anxious to talk about, and tell others about Jesus, whom they know is God.
h. Enjoys the company of others who love Jesus, so they seek a good church.
i. Begins to display the "fruit of the Spirit."
(Galatians 5:22-23 But the fruit of the Spirit is love, joy, peace, patience, kindness, goodness, faithfulness, gentleness and self-control.)

What is the definition of an unbeliever? Everybody else.

Notice that in contrast to the rituals that will make you accepted by other religions, this list deals only with issues of the heart—things that come from inside, as I Samuel 16:7b, mentioned previously, suggests.

Who gets to pick the metric?

I should take a moment to make a very important point here. Many people compare themselves to others and come to the conclusion that they are pretty good people. While that standard might be flattering for us, it is not God's standard. His standard is simple—*perfection*. If a person thinks they just might be perfect, they need only read through the Ten Commandments to test their prideful thinking.

The book that tells the future is unambiguous about this. It says in Romans 3:23, *"For ALL have sinned and come up short when measured by God's standard."* The standard for entering heaven is perfection. Since it's His heaven, it's His standard.

Every single sin must be paid for

The Bible says that all sin MUST be paid for— every single one. God is a perfectly righteous God and can't let sin go unpunished. If this wasn't true, then Jesus would not have needed to suffer the agony of the cross. But every single sin must be paid for one way or another. "One way or another" means either I pay for my sin, myself, or Jesus pays for it for me.

> *The standard for entering heaven is perfection. Since it's His heaven, it's His standard.*

I once left my car at an auto repair shop for some needed repair that I couldn't do myself. I received a call from the shop manager explaining that the repair was done, but that they noticed that I needed the brake pads replaced on the rear wheels.

Brake pad replacement is something I always do myself for a fraction of what they charge. I said, "No thank you." He pushed back a little, explaining that the wheels were already off the vehicle. I held firm. I sensed his irritation with my refusal.

The next month when I went to replace the brake pads myself, I found that they had put every single lug nut on so tightly that I literally twisted every bolt in half trying to get it off. I then had to remove and replace the broken bolts. This was not an accident. This was in retaliation for my refusal of their service.

I don't know who was responsible for that, but now, many years later, I'm sure they think they have gotten away with it. They haven't. You see, though I forgive them, every single sin must be paid for. Whoever did that will pay for it along with every other sinful thing they ever did or said or even thought, in their entire life. God's sense of perfect justice and righteousness demands it. The same thing goes for me and you *if not humbly repentant before God*—so says the book that tells the future.

Incidentally, for the uncontrite, their sin will one day be revealed for all the world to see because it was not covered by the blood of Jesus, who has the power to forgive sin and hide it forever. It will be a most embarrassing moment for the unrepentant.

Wives and husbands and mothers and friends and bosses and neighbors will all see what the sinner never wanted them to see. And yes, the book that tells the future says so. It can all be hidden, though, with a decision to follow Jesus, because His blood shed on the cross can forgive and hide that sin forever for those humbly repentant before God. The Bible says so.

You can pay the eternal consequences yourself, or…

The book that tells the future carefully explains that only the blood of Jesus, a perfectly innocent person, can pay the eternal consequences of a human being's sin. If a person decides not to follow Jesus, then that person will pay those consequences themself. Romans 6:23 says, *"The penalty for sin is eternal death, but the gift of God is eternal life, but only through Jesus Christ."*

> *Only the blood of Jesus, an innocent person, can pay the eternal consequences of a human being's sin—says the book that tells the future.*

This is the explanation of the only path to heaven described in the only book that tells the future. Sure, a person is free to bet on any other explanation of how to get there, but make no mistake, to do so one must bet against a book that tells the future.

Good deeds can never make up for bad deeds

Good deeds don't undo bad deeds. Contrary to popular opinion, the book that tells the future does not teach that good deeds get you INTO heaven. The Bible is very clear about the fact that it is *bad deeds* that disqualify you FROM heaven. And who doesn't have at least one—and one is all it takes. Just one sin makes you imperfect. Good deeds don't *qualify* you for heaven. Bad deeds *disqualify* you.

Even our laws have the same standard. You can be the nicest person in the world but if you rob a bank, you go to jail. Telling the judge all your good deeds will not make a difference.

Is it not shear arrogance to think you can get into God's heaven by your good works? Did Jesus not need to go to the cross? What was He thinking to have needlessly died, when you can get into His heaven on your own good behavior, alone? Don't you see how the idea that you can get into heaven on your good conduct must be highly insulting to Jesus who went to the cross for you?

> *Good deeds don't get you into heaven. Bad deeds keep you out.*

So, the dilemma for imperfect human beings is how to exchange their imperfection for the perfection necessary to ever enter heaven.

The Bible is not the least bit vague about how to do that. While all other religions tout good deportment as the way to get in, Jesus said this in John 14:6, "*I am the way, the truth and the life.* **Nobody will ever get into heaven except by me.**" Any questions?

Yes, the book that tells the future stands alone in its description of the path to heaven. How ironic that the spiritual path that says that good works will **not** get you into heaven is the same spiritual path that produces the most good works in the most generously charitable and genuinely philanthropic people on the planet! Yes, the people with the most good works are the same people that know that those good works won't get them into heaven. They know that only the blood of Jesus, shed to pay the consequences for their sin, can save their eternal souls.

Why, then, do they do the good works, if good works cannot get them into heaven? It is because Jesus changes people's hearts and gives them genuine love for others.

That love, though, is an enigma to unbelievers. They cannot explain it. They cannot comprehend the charity of the believing community expressed through their generous giving and endless sacrificial volunteer service in hospitals and prisons and food banks and orphanages the world over. They cannot fathom that believers represent the largest group of responders to natural disasters, far outpacing even the government. The Bible says it's because they don't know Jesus that they can't imagine such love.

> *Ironically, the people with the most good works are the same people that know that good works won't get them into heaven.*

Another example of the unbeliever's egregious inability to understand Christ-inspired love, is the comment of Ibram X. Kendi when he suggested that a family's loving adoption of ethnic children is just proof of their racism. The Washington post reported the comment, here: *https://www.washingtontimes.com/news/2020/sep/27/ibram-x-kendi-says-amy-coney-barrett-could-be-raci/*
This is clear evidence of the inability of many to comprehend the God-inspired compassion of people who love Jesus.

Eternity is in every human heart

Like a homing pigeon knows the way home, all human beings have an innate desire to connect with their Creator. Who can deny that when you consider all the different gods conjured up by all the different ethnic groups throughout all of history? It should be no wonder, though, since God tells us that He created us that way. Ecclesiastes 3:11 says, *"...He has also set eternity in the human heart."*

History shows that humans have always believed in the existence of the spiritual realm. Currently fulfilling Bible prophecy is evidence of God's existence. But the question arises, "What god is the true God and what path is the true path to Him?" As stated in the Introduction of this book, the devil has successfully confused the process with religious alternatives of every flavor to suit the palate.

Then, there are those who in their egotism would try to convince themselves that there is no God at all. They narcissistically think that they are unanswerable to anyone but themselves. Nevertheless, all societies throughout all of history have looked to some superior being or beings, invented or real, and have recognized their own inferiority before him, her, or them.

I have found that younger people seem to be a bit more open to spiritual matters. As people get older, they tend to come to some cozy opinion in their own mind, where they find a measure of comfort about God-related things. They can develop a false sense of security.

Even though their position is often based on little more than their own feelings or opinions, as some people get older they no longer feel a need or desire to discuss the matter. They lay down their bet and their final answer about all things spiritual and can be naively satisfied with it, yet they are unwilling and unprepared to defend it—a supremely foolish thing to do considering what is at stake.

Playing pretend / Making up your own reality.

> *They lay down their bet about all things spiritual and are foolishly good with it; they are even unwilling and unprepared to defend it.*

Let me tell you about my dear friend Malcolm. I met him around the year 2000 while working on a contract at an international corporation with offices in Houston. Everyone loved Malcolm. He was the nicest guy you could ever hope to meet.

Malcolm and I were assigned to work on the same project. At lunch, we would have stimulating conversations. In his pleasant British accent, he explained to me how he believed in reincarnation. I asked him the simple question, "Based on what?" His answer startled me when he said, "I don't know. I guess it just sounds logical to me." I couldn't believe that he was willing to bet his eternity on, "I don't know. I guess it just sounds logical to me."

There is more to the story. About that time, his doctor discovered that Malcolm had an aneurysm. He went into the hospital to have it repaired. A week later he was scheduled to be released. That day, however, something went very wrong and he died that evening. There had been a complication with his surgery. Unknown to the doctors, he had been bleeding internally all week long.

Sadly, I didn't know then what I know now about currently fulfilling Bible prophecy. Oh, I tried to discuss spiritual things with him, but I never seemed to get through to him the importance and trustworthiness of the Bible and its Gospel message.

> *In his pleasant English accent, he explained that he believed in reincarnation. I asked him the simple question, "Based on what?"*

This idea that you can believe whatever you want to believe, is true only up to a point—the point of death—because after that you don't get to make the rules anymore. Such people might be described in Isaiah 28:15 which says, *"So, you're happy with your understanding of the hereafter and you think you have nothing to worry about? How silly you are. Do you really think there is refuge in believing a lie? You've made self-deception your little hiding place."*

> *This idea that you can believe whatever you want is only true up to a point, because after death you don't get to make the rules, anymore.*

The truth, described in the book that tells the future, is an immovable object. No amount of willful rejection of it, or contempt for it, will change it one iota. There is literally no stopping it. A person who believes they can create their own eternal reality makes me

think of the urban-legend-exchange between a US naval captain and certain Canadian authorities off the coast of Newfoundland in October, 1995.
Americans: *Please divert your course 15 degrees to the north to avoid a collision.*
Canadians: *Recommend you divert YOUR course 15 degrees to the south to avoid a collision.*
Americans: *This is the captain of a US Navy ship. I say again, divert YOUR course.*
Canadians: *No. I say again, you divert YOUR course.*
Americans: *This is the aircraft carrier USS Lincoln, the second largest ship in the United States' Atlantic fleet. We are accompanied by three destroyers, three cruisers and numerous support vessels. I demand that YOU change your course 15 degrees north, that's one five degrees north, or countermeasures will be undertaken to ensure the safety of this ship.*
Canadians: *This is a lighthouse. Your call.*

When firm belief is not based on truth or on a book that tells the future, it assumes untold risk. A person has the right to believe whatever they like. All choices, though, come with consequences if not solidly based on truth.

Black Lives Matter

In August of 2020, Black Lives Matter protestors burned Bibles and, of course, the American flag in Portland, Oregon. I assume that not all supporters of BLM would endorse such a thing, but the videos on *YouTube* show no one objecting.

I bring this up to show the disrespect, even hatred, for the God of the Bible that exists in society. No other religious book was burned. Can you imagine if it had been a Koran? Equally disturbing was the New York Times reporting of the incident.

When the clear videos began to appear, The New York Times felt forced to say something. They could only comment on the videos, because they had no reporters physically present during the atrocity. This is how they chose to report it, weeks later, on August 11th, 2020: "A few protesters among the many thousands appear to have burned a single Bible — and possibly a second — for kindling to start a bigger fire. None of the other protesters seemed to notice or care."

Sure, you know how it is. Whenever you go camping—or in this case, to violent demonstrations that destroy entire communities—you always take a Bible or two with you in case you might need to start a fire. In The New York Times' attempt to minimize and downplay the matter, they unknowingly highlighted the atrociousness when they wrote that, *"None of the other protesters seemed to notice or care."* As far as they could tell from the video, no one seemed to care that Bibles were being burned.

You do not find such bitter loathing of any other religion. And why should you? The devil only hates the God of the Bible. The rest serve him nicely as decoys luring people away from the truth.

The devil loves religion. He just hates the one that teaches people that they can have a personal relationship with their Creator. He just hates the one that can save people from having to pay the eternal consequences for their sin themselves. He just hates the one that can rescue people from spending eternity with him.

> *The devil only hates the God of the Bible. The rest serve him nicely as decoys.*

I find it so sad that this repudiation of God is not limited to just some atheistic activist minority. Regrettably, there are many people who silently carry this derision for the God of the Bible.

> *The devil loves religion. He just hates the one that can rescue people from spending eternity with him.*

You should not be shocked to find there will always be those who will roll their eyes at any mention of God, the Bible, Jesus, or Christianity. It is reflective of an apparent contempt for those things.

As a matter of fact, the Bible goes out of the way to explain this truth at least three different ways with verses like Matthew 6:24 that contrasts **haters and lovers**, "*No one can serve two masters, for either he will hate the one and love the other, or he will be devoted to the one and despise the other.*"

Then, Matthew 25:32-34, 41 contrasts **sheep and goats**, "*All the nations will be gathered before him, and he will separate the people one from another as a shepherd separates the sheep from the goats. He will put the sheep on his right and the goats on his left. Then the King will say to* *those on his right, 'Come, you who are blessed by my Father'; ...then he will say to those on his left, 'Depart from me, you who are cursed.'"*

And finally, how about the contrast of **weeds and wheat** in Matthew 13:30, *"...and at harvest time I will tell the reapers, 'Gather the weeds first and bind them in bundles to be burned, but gather the wheat into my barn.'"*

When you are at the door of heaven seeking entrance, you certainly wouldn't want to hear the Lord say, "What did you think I meant when I said, *'I am the Way. I am the Truth. I am the Life. And nobody will ever enter these pearly gates except by Me.'"*

Those who resist God's truth are exposed when confronted by currently fulfilling Bible prophecy. They have no answer for how a book can tell the future, but they still have no interest in its message. These are people looking for any excuse not to believe.

I remember speaking to a colleague while on a contract job at an international corporation in Pennsylvania. I described currently fulfilling prophecies to him, but he was unreceptive and seemed uncomfortable with the subject, so I dropped the topic.

> *Haters are exposed when they have no answer for how a book can tell the future, but they still have no interest in its message.*

I wanted, though, to leave him with a thought that might help him to be open to the truth of the Bible at some later date. I commented that the Bible also spoke of things that have not yet occurred. I told him that the Bible, in Isaiah 17, is pretty clear that Damascus, the oldest, continuously inhabited city in the world, would be destroyed one evening and would never be rebuilt. I admitted that while I did not know exactly when that would happen, there was a chance that it could happen in his lifetime given the turmoil over there.

His reaction was, "That's the dumbest thing I've ever heard," to which I responded, "Exactly! So, when it happens, it will be noteworthy, right?" I'll never forget his response when he said, "Well, um, uh, actually I guess anything is possible."

Yes, there are those who hate anything that might validate the existence of God or the relevance of the Bible. That same hostility towards the Gospel is evident in movies, TV programs, work environments, schools, governments, and throughout society in general.

Yeah, and what about evolution?

When anyone goes to a magic show and watches the magician pull a dove out of a hat, they know that it's slight-of-hand. No one thinks it's real. Yet how silly is it that people are willing to accept the notion that the incredible complexity of the universe was formed from nothing at all—and without a creator.

The well-known atheist and biologist, Dr. Richard Dawkins, though he goes to all lengths to conjure arguments against the existence of God, unintentionally admitted this in his book *The*

Blind Watchmaker: "Biology is the study of complicated things that give the appearance of having been designed for a purpose."

So, let me get this straight, doctor. You're saying that it looks like a duck, it walks like a duck, and it quacks like a duck, but it's not a duck. OK, I think I see where you're coming from, now.

Consider just this one tiny fact that displays the awesomeness and design of God's creation. As a baby develops in its mother's womb, how long does the umbilical cord need to be? Even accounting for baby movement, it doesn't need to be that long at all, but it is. Why is that? Because when delivery of that baby finally comes, that cord needs to be *way long*. So, it is.

There are literally billions of facts like that one that make the idea that this all happened by itself—and from nothing—axiomatically preposterous. So, since this all needs a creator, it's a bit silly to claim there isn't one.

It's a lot like all of these currently fulfilling Bible prophecies—apart from God, you've no way to explain them.

It amazes me

It amazes me how some people can be presented with the undeniable facts of a book that tells the future, and then react by saying, "Well, let me tell you my take on religion."

That is like commenting on 1 + 1 = 2, by saying, "Well, that's interesting, but let me tell you how I see it." There is no room for opinion when dealing with a book that tells the future; just like there is no room for opinion when dealing with basic mathematics. There is only submission to it. Anything else will have less than a good final outcome.

The people who would have that reaction are the same people that would read this book and think it was about religion, when it is not the least bit about religion. It is about each of us and our relationship with our Creator.

> *That is like commenting on 1 + 1 = 2, by saying, "Well, that's interesting, but let me tell you how I see it."*

I guess 1 Corinthians 2:14 is true when it says, *"The person without the Spirit does not accept the things that come from the Spirit of God but considers them foolishness **and cannot understand them because they are discerned only through the Spirit.**"* Only when a person opens their mind and heart to their Creator will He give them His Holy Spirit along with the special aptitude and perception necessary to grasp spiritual things.

A reason to believe

> *Only when a person opens their mind and heart to their Creator will He give them His Holy Spirit along with the perception necessary to grasp spiritual truth.*

Not everyone is hostile towards the Gospel. Though they are a minority, there are those whose hearts and minds are open. They have the desire to connect with their Creator, because God made us that way, and they are not so haughty as to ignore it. Remember what Ecclesiastes 3:11 says, *"...He has also set eternity in the human heart."*

These people are looking for a reason to believe. Currently fulfilling Bible prophecy can give them the confidence they need to know they have found the truth and to embrace the message of the Bible so that they can be saved from having to pay the eternal consequences of their sin themselves.

There are those looking for a **reason to believe** and there are those who are looking for any **excuse not to**. According to the Bible, there is no one in between. Thankfully, though, those looking for an excuse not to believe can sometimes become one of those looking for a reason to believe through the love and patience of believers and the work of the Holy Spirit in their heart. But that won't happen unless there is an openness towards the truth. God says this in Revelation 3:20, *"Behold, I stand at the door and knock. If anyone hears my voice and opens the door, I will come in to him and we can get to know each other."*

> *There are those looking for a reason to believe and there are those who are looking for any excuse not to.*

God is looking for followers who grow to genuinely love Him back, not just people who on an intellectual level recognize the logic, beauty, and trustworthiness of the Bible. God is not looking for people who keep Him at arms-length by stiff-arming Him with one arm while they pat Him on the back with the other. He is looking for those who will enthusiastically embrace Him with both arms. That's the relationship that He originally created us for, and then died on a cross for. He expects nothing less.

> God is looking for followers who grow to genuinely love Him back, not just people who on an intellectual level recognize the logic, beauty, and trustworthiness of the Bible.

Past prophecy vs. currently fulfilling prophecy

While the skeptic or the less informed person may not believe all the past fulfilled prophecies described in the Bible, currently fulfilling prophecy is a different matter. It cannot be so easily ignored by an honest person.

For example, there are over 300 prophecies in the Old Testament describing details of Jesus' lineage, birth, life, struggles, death, and resurrection. The uninformed person may not know enough to be able to accept that these prophecies were indeed written before the time of Christ. For lack of historical awareness of such archeological discoveries as the Qumran scrolls, they may try to say that the Old Testament prophecies about Jesus could have been written *after* the time of Christ. Or, ignorant of the writings of Josephus and other non-Biblical references to the crucifixion of Jesus, they may question that He ever existed at all.

While past fulfilled prophecy is precious to believers, many unbelievers may not be aware of the variety of evidences that validate those past-fulfilled prophecies. However, there can be no argument against currently fulfilling Bible prophecy which anyone can clearly see occurring today.

Some don't get it. Some don't want it.

A missionary friend of ours, Karen Klassen, shared the Gospel with a dying man. He was unreceptive. After rejecting the message, he commented with a chuckle, "Well, I guess I'm going to burn in hell forever."

It is not that he believed in hell and that he was going there, but rather that he scornfully thought the whole idea of hell was a laughable concept that existed only in the minds of religious fanatics.

And why should he believe? At that time, he had not yet seen hell for himself, nor had he ever met anyone who had. And, apparently, no one had ever confronted him with the evidence of currently fulfilling Bible prophecy that may have elicited some respect for the Bible and its message. An awareness of currently fulfilling Bible prophecy may have removed any basis for his cavalier attitude.

> *He scornfully thought the whole idea of hell was a laughable concept that existed only in the minds of religious fanatics.*

Of course, there are still those who would mock anyway. Their disdain for spiritual things betrays their hatred of God and their derision for His followers. At least that's what Jesus said in John 15:18, *"If the world hates you, remember that **it hated me first**."* And how about 1 Corinthians 1:18 which says, *"**The message of the cross is foolish to those who are headed for destruction**!"* Finally, what could be clearer than John 15:19 that reads, *"The world would love you as one of its own if you belonged to it, but you are no longer part of the world. I chose you to come out of the world, **so it hates you**."*

Nevertheless, when an honest person comes to understand that the events and conditions in the world around them were all foretold in the Bible to occur at this point in history, well, that is when they may be open to its beautiful message—the Gospel.

> *Their disdain for spiritual things betrays their hatred for God and their derision for His followers.*

Currently fulfilling prophecy is irrefutable evidence of the accuracy and miraculous nature of the Bible. No honest, rational person can deny the miracle of currently fulfilling prophecy that can be read in the Bible and can be observed occurring around them. That same rational person should then be at least a bit curious about the message of such a book.

Final Thoughts

Any Information Age believer today must have the utmost respect for the followers of Jesus from times past. Hundreds of years ago, it called for a huge measure of faith to believe the Bible when it spoke of the entire world simultaneously watching the same event or the Jews returning to Israel when it didn't even exist or the ability to control individual purchases worldwide. Today, we see the unmistakable fulfillment of all those prophecies and many others. Still more prophecies we can see developing on a close horizon as we watch the wave of world affairs and technology hurtle us uncontrollably forward.

Seeing is believing. Today, it hardly takes any faith at all to believe the Bible. There are so many currently fulfilling Bible prophecies that make the Bible's authenticity self evident. All that's needed to believe the Bible, is a little honesty about it all. And there's the problem...

Confirmation bias

In spite of all the currently fulfilling Bible prophecies that remove any doubt as to its credibility, there are many who will deliberately not accept it. This irrational and intentional ignoring of the obvious comes from a strong confirmation bias.

> *It hardly takes any faith today, to believe the Bible. There are so many currently fulfilling Bible prophecies that make the Bible's authenticity self-evident.*

Confirmation bias is defined this way: *...the tendency to search for, interpret, favor, and recall information that confirms or supports one's prior personal beliefs or values.*

The confirmation bias of those not willing to accept currently fulfilling prophetic facts can be much stronger than a simple "tendency" to be influenced by their prejudices. Because of the profound desire of some to not be bothered by God, it becomes a raging compulsion to abandon objectivity and yield to their confirmation bias.

By the way, to ever accuse followers of Jesus of having a confirmation bias is a bit silly. To do so would assume that Christians want to believe Romans 3:23 about themselves, which says, "**Everybody is a sinner** *and no one comes close to measuring up to God's standards.*" And Jeremiah 17:9 which says, "*The human heart is the most deceitful of all things, and* **desperately wicked**. *Who really knows how bad it is?*" And Mark 7:21-23 which says, "*For from within,* **out of the heart of men, proceed evil** *thoughts, adulteries, fornications, murders, thefts, covetousness, wickedness, deceit, lasciviousness, an evil eye, blasphemy, pride, foolishness: all these evil things come from within, and defile the man.*"

No one wants to think those things about themself. Confirmation bias would want to believe the opposite. People want to believe that they are basically good, not basically bad. Real believers, however, accept the Bible's negative description of human nature because, first of all, they are honest to admit that even casual objectivity must recognize the dark side in all of us, and second of all, a book that tells the future says so. None of this is the result of confirmation bias at all. It is just the result of simple honesty about the facts.

Back to the subject of confirmation bias against God. This unnatural contempt for God, the Bible, the mention of Jesus, etc., almost always comes from one particular type of person. It does not come from people of other religions, nor does it come from people with little or no religious experience.

People most prone to be uncomfortable with God-related discussions—who are they?

Most rejection of God comes from people who have had some exposure to religiosity that one day came to be uncomfortable for them. Their religious experience seemed empty, onerous, or laborious for them. Some may have felt that they suffered some real or perceived offense or injustice at the hands of religious people. In fact, it is not hard to believe that religious people who don't have a real relationship with Jesus could indeed be guilty of many offences and injustices.

These are most often adults whose parents took them to church. Unfortunately, they only saw religion. Religion is a huge turn-off. A real relationship with Jesus is something else entirely. And maybe they were never taught what a relationship with Jesus really looks like and they may not even understand what that means, (though they may think they do.) And, in most cases, they were never shown the overwhelming and irrefutable evidences for God and the Bible.

For them, church is little more than a dutiful activity that cultured people do. It isn't something that radically impacts their life. Besides, they may not even want that kind of outside interference.

I have the greatest pity for these people who have grown up in religious families and religious systems that were more about the system, traditions, and rituals, and less about a personal relationship with Jesus. Isaiah 29:13 describes these religious systems this way: *"The Lord says: 'These people come near to me with their mouth and honor me with their lips, but their hearts are far from me. **Their worship of me is made up only of rules taught by men**.'"*

> Church, for them, is little more than a dutiful activity that cultured people do. It isn't something that radically impacts their life.

Those who were raised in such systems saw the emptiness, the pride, the false piety, and demands of religion but never the beauty, the love, the compassion, the deep sense of purpose, the incredible confidence, and the profound hope and security that can only come from a genuine relationship with Jesus. If they don't end up abandoning church themselves, their children are sure to. There is always the hope, though, that someone will come to see past the religiosity of hollow religious tradition and develop a real personal relationship of their own with Jesus.

These are often the last people to figure it out. After all, in their minds, they think they have "been there and done that" when, in fact, they never saw the real thing at all. But they think they have, and it is difficult to convince them otherwise.

Their heart is not in a place to learn anything because their particular religious experience was so anticlimactic—maybe even hurtful. At best it was mostly empty.

> *They think they have "been there and done that" when, in fact, they never saw the real thing at all.*

They don't understand that it was spiritually meaningless because they were never shown, or never grasped, what a real relationship with Jesus looks like. They saw platitudes and high thought but not something that would touch the deepest part of their soul and transform them. In fact, that idea probably scares them a little.

These people remind me of a co-ed in an exchange with Albert Einstein. They happened to be sitting beside each other at a formal dinner. Not recognizing him, she asked what he did. He answered that he was "engaged in the study of physics." Her response? "Oh, I took that last semester." How naive she was to think that she had a true grasp of the profundities of physics like Albert Einstein had.

Many people from a religious background are like the co-ed with regard to spiritual things. They are oblivious to their own unawareness of what a true relationship with Jesus really looks like. Since they have only known empty religion, they find the very subject of spiritual things extremely uncomfortable. And so, they can even become hostile towards it. They are no longer open to the Gospel or a discussion of spiritual things.

> *They are oblivious to their own unawareness of what a true relationship with Jesus really looks like.*

It's a little hard to blame them, though, because all they have ever seen were the do's and don'ts of religiosity and not the delight, depth, and adventure of their own relationship with Jesus. So personal. So fulfilling. So empowering.

Many people know what it means to be religious—you know, go to church on Sunday and maybe put a little money in the offering plate. But a deep personal relationship with Jesus Christ is something beyond their experience and maybe a little beyond their comfort zone, as well.

What God created us for, and then died on a cross for us for, was so that we and He could be friends. You see, our sin blocks any real communication with a perfect Creator. Our sin must be paid for before communication can be restored. I couldn't pay for your sin because I've got my own to worry about. Only a perfect person like Jesus Christ could ever pay the consequences of our sin so that we wouldn't have to. But to be qualified for such a reprieve from the repercussions of sin, we must have a personal relationship with Jesus.

What's so hard to understand?

Why is it that one person can hear the facts of currently fulfilling Bible prophecy and be persuaded that this book deserves closer scrutiny, and another person can hear the very same facts, and although they cannot refute them, they have no curiosity whatsoever about the message of such a book?

Even more perplexing is how one person can be overwhelmed to the point of tears in appreciation for the message that describes a patient and loving God that bore the eternal consequences for their sin; while another person can hear the same message of love from a book that tells the future, even, and not be moved at all?

Smooth sailing was yesterday's news, not tomorrow's

This rejection of God should come as no surprise, though, because another currently fulfilling Bible prophecy in Matthew 24:10 warns us that it would be so, with these words, "*At that time **many will turn away from the faith**....*" This has already begun, and we know that it will only get worse. Many churches hardly stand for anything anymore. As they have gone soft on what the Bible says, their congregations have gone, too. And why wouldn't the congregations disappear as the churches become little more than community centers, forfeiting any eternal spiritual relevance.

All these currently fulfilling Bible prophecies are portents of an approaching day of reckoning. In fact, the severe and troublesome circumstances that the world is helplessly sinking into these days has a lot of people thinking that day of reckoning may be closer than we thought.

> *All these currently fulfilling Bible prophecies are portents of an approaching day of reckoning.*

There may be times coming when a person will not survive without a faith that is personal, proven, and empowering—and based on verifiable truth, not emotions, changing social conventions or opinions.

At that time, there will be no hiding behind your own opinions and philosophies that for many includes a "personally engineered spirituality" they claim to have. Personal beliefs born of one's own intellect, prejudice, or confirmation bias will seem embarrassingly hollow and without solution when facing a world out of control. The book that tells the future warns us it will be so.

God's truth is no mystery, however, to those who have taken the Bible seriously. Their study of the book that tells the future informs them of exactly what will happen when that time comes. They are prepared. At that time, the truth will finally be obvious to everyone, but the regrets will be profound for those not prepared.

Anything but God

Of course, there are also those whose rejection of God is not the result of ignorance about Him but is rather due to a pride and absolute unwillingness to humble themself before God. It is a result of loving their sin and their independence from God more than anything else.

I'll recount for you just such an encounter. I was in a country where foreigners are forbidden to share the Gospel.

One of my destinations was a very poor rural area where there was a humble country church with about 200 members. This church had a hugely positive influence on the small town, with nearly 40% of its residents regularly attending.

> *There are those whose rejection of God is the result of loving their sin and their independence from God more than anything else.*

The pastor took me around to meet everyone. I visited the humble homes of the members to encourage them. I also visited the homes of those who did not attend church. I shared currently fulfilling Bible prophecy with them so that they would have a respect for the Bible before I shared the Gospel with them. Many, accepted. This story is about one who didn't.

He was about 35 years old. He seemed to listen patiently as I enumerated the Bible prophecies that were currently being fulfilled in the world around him. Then I shared the beautiful Gospel—the story of God's love for us. I explained how God, being perfectly righteous, is obligated to punish all sin. I told him that God, though, in His love, found a way to save us from having to pay the eternal consequences of our sin ourselves.

I described how Jesus, being an innocent person, died in our place, and that God was now just looking for people that would genuinely love Him back. I asked him if he wanted to do that. He said, "No."

I asked him to help me understand why not. I told him how I had shared this important message with thousands of people and that while many responded affirmatively, there were some, like him, who didn't. I wanted to try to understand how a proven story of love rescuing the lost could be ignored, especially when it came from a book that undeniably tells the future.

> *I told him that God was just looking for people that would genuinely love him back. I asked him if he wanted to do that. He said, "No."*

I asked him if he had some explanation for how a book could tell the future. He said, "No." I continued by reminding him that this book that tells the future, which only God can do, explains to us the eternal consequences of sin as well as the protection from those consequences that is available through Jesus. I explained that God offers impunity to anyone who would love Him back for bearing their sin on the cross. I asked him what was wrong with that beautiful picture.

He said, "Nothing", but that he did not want to follow Jesus. This was in February of 2017. I was back in that same village eight months later in October of the same year. I asked the pastor about this man. The pastor's face saddened as he told me the unhappy story.

It turns out that his 6-year-old daughter came home from school one day to find her dad swinging in the doorway by a rope around his neck. His little girl didn't realize he was dead as she cried, "Daddy, come down from there. Don't play like that. It's not funny!"

Maybe God knew that under no circumstances was this man ever going to humble himself before Him. So, He stepped back from protecting him from the devil, who the Bible tells us wants always to destroy us. If God didn't protect us, the devil would have already done away with us all. The devil loves it when an unbeliever dies, because then there is no risk that they might accept Jesus and escape his grasp. Remember, it is a book that tells the future that carefully explains this all to us.

> His 6-year-old daughter came home from school one day to find her dad swinging in the doorway by a rope around his neck.

I heard another story about a similar person who eschewed spiritual things. He was an athlete on a baseball team. He told a teammate that he would be gone from practice the next day because he was going in for his annual checkup after having had cancer years earlier. His confidence was high because there had been nary a trace of it for ten years.

His teammate was a Christian and asked him if he wanted him to "hope" things would go well or "pray" things would go well. The baseball player responded with a snicker that both were equally superstitious. The Christian knew his prayers would be of no avail because of his teammate's lack of faith, so he said that he would at least "hope" for the best.

The baseball player's checkup revealed that the cancer had returned aggressively, and he died within six months. I wonder if before he passed away he ever questioned his scorn for God, or thought to himself, "What would it have hurt to have asked my Christian friend to pray for me?"

What's your final answer?

When a person's final answer is to reject God, God respectfully honors their wishes to spend eternity without the presence God or any of the people who follow Him. The book that tells the future explains that they will endure all of eternity away from the presence of God and away from all that is good, where they must suffer the eternal consequences for every bad thing they ever did. The sad part is that it doesn't have to be like that since Jesus painstakingly made a way to escape.

> *When a person's final answer is to reject God, He respectfully leaves them alone for all of eternity.*

The book that tells the future says there is a heaven and a hell. To assume otherwise is foolhardy and irresponsibly reckless, because it ignores the warnings of the only book that tells the future.

I must admit to being completely mystified when I see a person make self-destructive decisions that reject truth, logic, and love, and instead choose a path of eternal suffering that is clearly warned against in the incontestable book that tells the future. This is an anomaly that makes no sense at all.

If it is not true, you lose nothing
But if it is true, you lose everything

After all, where is the risk in following Jesus even if you are wrong (except, of course, for the intolerance you can expect to experience from people hostile to the God of the Bible). On the other hand, rejecting Jesus incurs incalculable and eternal risk if you are wrong. And furthermore, to do so you must bet against a book that tells the future.

What can make you blind to truth?

I think I know how people can become so dismissive of the facts and so unresponsive to spiritual truth, even in light of the unpleasant consequences for doing so. It is an extreme case of confirmation bias that doesn't like what the facts are showing. I know it's an uncomfortable suggestion, but isn't it really just arrogant self-will that resists humility before God?

> *Rejecting Jesus incurs incalculable and eternal risk if you are wrong.*

There is a remedy for this condition, though. It is found in Ezekiel 36:26 where God says, "*I will give you a new heart and put a new spirit in you; I will remove from you your heart of stone and give you a heart of flesh.*"

God said this to the Jews, explaining how their hearts would finally change when one day they all accept Jesus as the Messiah. But the same process happens to anyone who decides to follow Jesus.

Some people, however, just don't want to have to think about it. Though currently fulfilling Bible prophecy is proof positive that the Bible is a supernatural book without equal they have difficulty accepting its message because they'll have to do something.

It's like someone being offered ten million dollars and being unwilling to accept it because there will be taxes to pay and investments to make. It brings new responsibilities that they don't want to have to worry about. And besides that, other people may be jealous of them and not like them. But considering all that, don't you still have to come to the conclusion that it's worth it? Of course.

It is even more so with the message of the Bible. Sure, there are responsibilities that come along with it. And yes, there will be people who don't like you; and there's much to learn about what a relationship with your Creator really means. But what could be of more value than eternal life and freedom from having to pay the eternal consequences of your sin, yourself? Don't you still have to come to the conclusion that it's worth it? Of course.

What's your purpose?

God stuff is a lot like IRS stuff for a lot of people. It's something that they know they are going to have to deal with, at some point, but they want to delay that moment as long as possible. When a person thinks like that, they have fallen prey to the devil's suggestion that God's way lacks excitement or is boring. Nothing could be further from the truth.

My life certainly hasn't been boring. It includes face to face threats from sicarios and surprise confrontations with alligators and the deadliest snakes in Latin America. Did I mention falling over a waterfall or navigating alone through primitive jungles with real threats all around, or setting up pirate radio stations that are preaching the Gospel 24/7 in remote areas in foreign countries? Or how about stealthily entering countries closed to the Gospel, then boldly preaching there as you carefully stay ahead of the authorities who would throw you out, if they could catch you? Maybe you wouldn't want such experiences. Maybe they seem more scary than adventurous to you. But guess what…?

That's the neat thing! God knows you better than you know yourself and the life that is dedicated to him will be the most fulfilling and purposeful life ever as God leads you in the best way for you, to bring fulfillment, purpose and value into your life.

> *Or how about stealthily entering countries closed to the Gospel?*

The madness of marginalizing God

The idea that God can be ignored or marginalized is such a simple-minded notion. It's difficult to imagine such insolent bravado, against the creator of the universe, coming from a mere spec on this tiny planet circling in this undersized solar system of the vast Milky Way that represents nearly nothing of the endless universe. How intellectually pretentious, even conceited, not to mention brash and puerile, to dismiss the Creator of the entire universe, based on one's painfully limited knowledge and life-experience on this little orb of the limitless cosmos.

We mustn't mistake God's love, patience and mercy for weakness or impotence. He gives plain warning of His coming final judgement on those who rebuff Him in 2 Peter 2:4-9 that says, *"For if God did not spare angels when they sinned, but sent them to hell, putting them in chains of darkness to be held for judgment; if he did not spare the ancient world when he brought the flood on its ungodly people; ...if he condemned the cities of Sodom and Gomorrah by burning them to ashes, and made them an example of what is going to happen to the ungodly; ...if this is so, then the Lord knows how to rescue the godly from trials and to hold the unrighteous for punishment on the day of judgment."*

It should be remembered that these cannot be easily ignored as empty words if they come from a book that clearly and irrefutably tells the future. And if you are tempted to think God is somehow harsh or unfair, remember that He died for you. When a person dies for you, you can't say that they haven't done enough for you. Yes, God is love, but God is righteous, too. He cannot tolerate sin—which is people hurting themselves or others.

God is not impotent

Could God not stop the rain or cause it to constantly rain if He wanted to? Could He not stop all wind and breezes or allow tornadoes and hurricanes constantly? Could He not let meteors fall or constant earthquakes to occur? Could He not allow plagues, pestilences, and disease that would persecute or even annihilate humanity, if

He wanted to do so? Who do you think controls those things? When God wanted to cover the earth with water, He warned everyone that He was going to do it. Then, when no one took Him seriously, He just did it. Seashells on the highest mountains prove it's true, as do a myriad of other evidences.

How shallow to not realize the truth of Acts 17:28 which says, *"For in him we live and move and exist."* Lucky for all of us, He loves us. Even the ones that refuse to love Him back. His patience gives us time to get our thinking straight.

> When He wanted to cover the earth with water, He just did it. Seashells on the highest mountains prove it's true.

God has kept all the plates spinning so that seasons occur on schedule and temperatures remain within limits and humanity is not decimated by plagues or disease. Sure, occasionally God allows things to happen to remind us He is there when we start to take Him for granted.

But God has allowed the worldwide economy to improve dramatically over the last 100 years. The world has never seen the prosperity it enjoys today. He has allowed science and technology to make people's lives easier. Yet, all these blessings have only served to cause most people to be less God-conscious as they foolishly think that either He has nothing to do with their prosperity or that there are no consequences for ignoring Him or that He does not exist, at all.

Impossible to please

Just before Jesus returns to clean up the mess that man is making of it all, He is going to let many of those plates spin down and crash. It will be hard to ignore Him then. Even so, rather than repent, people will curse God, the Bible tells us in Revelation 16:9b which says, *"they cursed the name of God, who had control over all these plagues. They did not repent of their sins and turn to God and give him glory."*

God has blessed the world to unprecedented levels of prosperity and people have ignored Him. When that prosperity is compromised and God begins to allow the world to reap what it has been sowing, people will still ignore Him. But even more than ignore Him, they will show their contempt for Him all-the-more, as the verse above tells us.

> *God has kept all the plates spinning, but He is going to let many of them spin down and crash. It will be hard to ignore Him then.*

It is a little like it was in Jesus' day. How frustrated He must have felt when He said this in Matthew 11:16-19, *"How can I explain this generation? It is like children that might say to their playmates, 'We played happy songs for you, and you did not dance; so we played sad songs, but you wouldn't mourn, either.'*

Because John the Baptist came neither eating nor drinking, and they said, 'He has a demon.' Then I came along both eating and drinking, and they say, 'Look at him! A glutton and a drunkard, a friend of lowlifes and street people'."

There is just no pleasing those determined to spurn God. Give them wealth and they ignore Him. Take it away and they blame Him.

There are more and more real students of the Bible who are beginning to think that the time is getting very near when God is going to force man to acknowledge Him by stepping back from keeping everything under control, and by starting to let humanity reap the consequences of its rejection of Him.

> There is just no pleasing those determined to spurn God. Give them wealth and they ignore God. Take it away and they blame God.

At some point, God will stop being an "enabler" by keeping the plates all spinning. At some point, He will let man's antagonism and rejection of righteousness begin to feel its due repercussions. It is beginning to seem like that time may be getting closer.

Approaching critical mass

I recently spoke with a friend about the social state of America. He has given no indication that he is the least bit religious, yet he was very exercised as he described to me the destructive forces that are becoming increasingly evident in society. He explained that America seems to be going places from where it will most likely not recover. This seemingly unreligious man suggested how

> At some point God will stop being an "enabler" by keeping the plates all spinning.

appropriate for today was the Barry McGuire song entitled, "Eve of Destruction".

If the immorality, corruption, selfishness, egotism, violence, and absence of compassion in this world has gotten to the point that it is discernable and disconcerting even to some unbelievers, what must God think of it all? Do you really believe that He is going to sit idly by and watch the complete destruction of His creation and the total victory of evil over good? I tell you He won't. But the book that tells the future says that He will let it get to the brink.

> *This apparently unreligious man suggested how appropriate for today was the Barry McGuire song entitled, "Eve of Destruction".*

We are coming into a time when, more than ever, you need an anchor to keep you from losing it. Every person alive is looking for peace and security. Some of the places people look are money, power, money, sex, money, food, money, drugs, money, government, and even money. Oh, did I mention money? Just how do you think that is going to work out for them in the end?

There can be no excuse since the book that tells the future distinctly warns us that this security can only be found in a personal relationship with Jesus.

Honesty and...

I have spoken of the honesty necessary to discern truth, since one must resist their confirmation bias in order to be completely objective about the facts of currently fulfilling Bible prophecy. But there is something else that is critical to ever getting it right about spiritual things. It's another word related to honesty that also starts with the letter 'h'. The word is *humility*. Here is where the truth of the Bible loses a lot of folks.

Humility goes against human nature and even more so against western culture human nature. Some people are willing to embrace most of the truth we read about in the book that tells the future. But for some "humility" is a *bridge too far*. It is a critical element of salvation that some people *just can't handle*. It cannot be overstated that while Jesus made a way for men's souls to be rescued, by His sacrifice on the cross, no one will ever appropriate that hope for themself without humility before God.

Americans and most first world citizens are a difficult mission field for the Gospel of the Bible because of a pride that is more like an arrogance. Who can deny it when you see our present-day culture with such delicate sensitivities that are so easily offended? People no longer react against others for their actions, but now simply for their words. To be completely honest, not only for their words, but for what we *assume* are the motives behind the words. Yes, society wants to judge people for what it supposes people are thinking.

> *Humility is a "bridge too far." It is a critical element of salvation that many people just can't handle.*

While many used to be guilty of 'wearing their feelings on their sleeves,' their feelings are now a huge bubble that surrounds them, making them hypersensitive to the least—and even unintentional—provocation. Road rage, petty lawsuits, "safe zones," unforgiveness, violent demonstrations, extreme selfishness, entitled behavior and easily fractured relationships everywhere betray this ugly hubris to be true.

It is not very likely that type of person would ever be introspective, objective or humble enough to ever grasp the simple and unpretentious Gospel.

Now that's humility!

Consider this encounter that Jesus once had with a woman soliciting him for a favor. We find the account in Matthew 15:21-28. *"Then Jesus left Galilee and went north to the region of Tyre and Sidon. A Gentile woman who lived there came to him, pleading, 'Have mercy on me, O Lord, Son of David! For my daughter is possessed by a demon that torments her severely.' But Jesus gave her no reply, not even a word. Then his disciples urged him to send her away. 'Tell her to go away,' they said. 'She is bothering us with all her begging.' Then Jesus said to the woman, 'I was sent only to help God's lost sheep—the people of Israel.' But she came and worshiped him, pleading again, 'Lord, help me!' Jesus responded, 'It isn't right to take food from the children and throw it to the dogs.' She replied, 'That's true, Lord, but even dogs are allowed to eat the scraps that fall beneath their master's table.'*

'Oh! woman,' Jesus said to her, 'Your faith is great! Your request is granted.' And her daughter was instantly healed."

Can you imagine that encounter happening today? When Jesus first ignored her, most people would have left, recounting the story of Jesus' rudeness.

Then his disciples suggested He run her off. Jesus was not about to do that because He actually had a plan based on a deep compassion for her that we will see in a moment.

When she persisted, Jesus finally responded to her, but with an off-putting comment when He said that He was a Jew sent only to the Jews. This recognition of her presence, though, only emboldened her to repeat her request. Jesus followed, then, with what would certainly be an insult today, and must have been so even then, when He said, *"It isn't right to take food from the children and throw it to the dogs."* With that remark you would expect her to be insulted and enraged, but she wasn't when she responded, *"... even dogs are allowed to eat the scraps..."*

> When Jesus first ignored her, most people would have left, recounting the story of Jesus' rudeness.

Finally, we see the compassion that Jesus was hiding as He feigned the opposite while He tested her heart. He not only granted her the miracle she sought but profoundly complimented her faith.

Even more than that, He communicated His deepest admiration for her. She knew it when Jesus used the exclamatory Greek word translated as *"Oh!".* Strong's Concordance defines this Greek word like this:

5599 (an exclamatory particle) – Oh!
5599 /ō ("oh!") **always expresses intense emotion**. *Depending on the context,*
5599 (ō) can convey: **spirited approval**, *urgency, exasperation, importance, joy, etc.*

I expect his disciples all stopped in their tracks and thought, "Did a Jewish rabbi really just say that to a Gentile woman?" To the Jewish culture of the day, there were "mere women" and then even lower on the social scale there were "mere Gentile women". But not to Jesus.

A person's reaction to circumstances usually betrays their heart. Jesus was giving her the opportunity to show her pure and humble heart. Of course, Jesus knew perfectly well what her reaction would be. He allowed her a test that would give her an immediate blessing in the healing of her daughter and an eternal reward as well.

> *To the Jewish culture of the day there were mere women and then even lower on the social scale there were mere Gentile women. But not to Jesus.*

He also gave her every opportunity to embrace an excuse to ignore Him altogether, if she so chose. But her pure heart was not going there; she wanted a touch from Jesus no matter what.

That encounter was a learning experience for his disciples, as it should be even today for us.

How many of us would have miserably failed that test?

What's your excuse?

If a person is looking for an excuse to reject God, they will always find one. I would even say that God, like with the woman in the parable, will afford a person the opportunity to embrace an excuse if that is what they want. You see, God is looking for those who will genuinely love Him back. Excuses separate the true lovers from the rest.

Those looking for an excuse not to believe are easy to spot. You won't find them reading books like <u>A Case for Christ</u> by Lee Strobel or <u>Mere Christianity</u> by C. S. Lewis, or <u>The Reason for God</u> by Timothy Keller, which make ignoring God impossible with persuasive arguments that would convince any objective and honest jury. No, instead you will find them reading anything else that might give them an excuse not to believe.

So many people rush to embrace the excuse when tested. The most popular excuse in the world is "hypocrites in the church" of course. When a person stands before God, as the book that tells the future promises we all will, how sad for those that show up with excuses like that one.

What they are likely to hear is this, *"That was actually a test to see if you would look past the hypocrisy that you saw around you and reach for Me, or if instead you would embrace the excuse and use it as your reason to ignore Me."*

When they come into God's court with the excuse of "hypocrites in the church", they will find that the very thing that they expected would be their defense will lamentably only serve to indict them. It will plainly show their choice to embrace the excuse instead of Jesus.

> *That was actually a test to see if you would look past the hypocrisy around you and reach for Me.*

The way to God's heart

We can learn something here about how to get God's ear. King David knew the secret, as well, after he had committed adultery and murder. Just one part of his prayer of repentance you can read in Psalm 51:16-17 that says. *"You do not desire a sacrifice, or I would offer one. You do not want a burnt offering. The sacrifice you desire is a humble spirit.* **You will not reject a broken and repentant heart, O God**.*"*

Another explicit verse is James 4:6 which says, *"God opposes the proud but shows favor to the humble."* In Isaiah 66:2, God is very clear about what kind of person He responds to when He says, *"...but to this man will I look, even to him that is of a poor and contrite spirit, and who is highly respectful of my word."*

If you were to put that verse in your own words you might say, *"I'll tell you the kind of person that I'm going to respond to. It certainly isn't going to be smug arrogant types or the prideful. It's going to be the person with a humble heart that takes me and my words very seriously."*

One final thing

There is this perception among many that one's choice of spiritual path is like picking a team to root for. While it might be that way for any other spiritual path, the one described in the book that tells the future demands more than a team jersey. It calls for a heart transplant. That is a surgery that you cannot perform on yourself, but God can, if you let Him.

God wants us to be prepared for His return or our own passing, whichever comes first. It doesn't make much sense to invest so much effort and preparation into a comfortable life and retirement, but just *hope* for the best when it comes to eternity.

Eternity is undeniably real because we have a book that undeniably tells the future that says so. God wants the very best for us. So, He gives us some really good advice in Proverbs 3:5 & 6 which says, *"Learn to trust in the Lord with all your heart. Don't make the mistake of thinking you're smarter than God. Consider Him in all your decisions and He'll help you to make the wisest choices throughout your life."*

> *The book that tells the future demands more than a team jersey. It calls for a heart transplant.*

Is it logical for a person to recognize the authenticity of currently fulfilling Bible prophecy yet ignore the message of such a book? To recognize the authenticity of Bible prophecy is to then be faced with the authenticity of its message, as well.

Recognizing the Bible's legitimacy happens in your head. Submitting to its message happens in your heart. Many, at this point, decide to have a little chat with Jesus, thanking Him for dying in their place and apologizing for having offended Him with their sin. When they ask Him for forgiveness and to take control of the rest of their life, He promises to put His Holy Spirit in them, giving them a whole new perspective on life as well as a new aptitude for eternal truth.

Additionally, there is a peace that floods a person's mind and heart at that point. That's because the promise of Philippians 4:6-7 is now theirs when it says, *"Do not be anxious about anything, but in every situation, by prayer and petition, with thanksgiving, present your requests to God. And the peace of God, which transcends all understanding, will guard your hearts and your minds in Christ Jesus."*

Closing Notes

I sincerely hope that this book has been a blessing to you. If you are already a believer, then you should be encouraged, knowing that your faith is defended by an undeniably miraculous book. Eternal truth is on your side with a book that proves itself by telling the future. Be emboldened, now, to share this truth that *everybody ought to know*.

If you are not a believer, the adventure of a very personal relationship with your own Creator awaits you. A little humility and a little honesty is all it takes. For eternity you will thank yourself. A book that tells the future says so.

Contact the author
Feel free to contact the author at dan@gamwell.com

Share your opinion
If you enjoyed this book, please leave a review at: amazon.com and goodreads.com

Make a difference in the lives of others.
This book would make an excellent gift for anyone who is searching for answers or that may just need reassurance, encouragement, or inspiration.

If you want to purchase multiple copies of Everybody Ought to Know, for evangelism efforts, please contact the author at dan@gamwell.com *Very significant discounts are available.*

Acknowledgments

While there was no single editor of this book, there were a number of capable people who read this book and offered suggestions that have made it what it is.

That list would include Paul Wicker, Mario Rodriguez, Merrily Gamwell, Deb Neall, Kevin Ikle, Kurt Nauck, Mike Vinton, Sue Kaiser, Tom Gamwell, Charlene Mundy and others. I thank God for each of them and their sacrificial contribution.

I must earnestly thank Dr. David Reagan and Lamb and Lion Ministries that have greatly influenced the content of this book.

I am also very appreciative of Nancy Sylvester for her kind and encouraging comments on the rear cover. Her book, "You're More Than Dirt", is a beautiful allegory that will touch the heart of any reader and open their eyes to a brighter and more confident perspective of their own life. It is available on Amazon.com.

www.ingramcontent.com/pod-product-compliance
Lightning Source LLC
LaVergne TN
LVHW051552070426
835507LV00021B/2547